NEYMAR
The Wizard

D0325263

NEYMAR
The Wizard

By

Michael Part

Sole BOOKS

A special thank you to Yonatan Ginsberg for his contribution to this
book. His love and depth of knowledge of the beautiful game were
invaluable. Special thanks to Yaron and Guy Ginsberg.

Research: Nilce Sousa.
Cover design: Omer Pikarski
Front cover photo: REUTERS/Ueslei Marcelino
Back cover photo: AP Photo/André Penner
Series editor: Y Ginsberg
Proof editor: Michele Caterina
Page layout design: Lynn M. Snyder
Library of Congress Cataloging-in-Publication data available.

ISBN: 978-193859-11-98

Published by Sole Books, Beverly Hills, California
Printed in the United States of America
First edition August 2014

10987654321

www.solebooks.com

To Dave & Heather Van Loan

The Smile

Neymar da Silva Santos Senior's car reached the top of the mountain and he aimed it downhill. His wife, Nadine, sat in the front seat and his infant son, Neymar da Silva Santos Junior, was in a crib strapped into the backseat. When Neymar Junior was born, Neymar Senior became *Pai* and they called Neymar Junior, *Juninho*. *Pai* meant *father* in Portuguese and Juninho meant *little junior.* They had left their home in Mogi das Cruzes, just east of São Paulo city, to visit Pai's parents on the coast.

Pai liked the rain. He figured they could make good time since the storm would keep most people indoors. His parents lived in São Vicente, in a house he bought them with the money he had earned playing professional soccer. He also bought himself a car. *This* car.

He was thinking about the match he had just played. He scored a goal for his team, Uniao Mogi. Nadine and Juninho were in the stands, watching him play. After the game, a boy he knew from the neighborhood had rushed up to him with a ball, asked for his autograph, and told him he thought he was the greatest soccer player in the world. It moved Pai. He told the boy he hoped his baby boy Juninho inherited his skills on the pitch.

Going downhill and picking up speed, Pai tensed when he saw a car coming straight at them on the wrong side of the road. He flashed his bright lights but the rain was so thick the other driver did not see them until it was too late. Pai cranked the wheel over and ran himself off the road, flooring it, hoping he could avoid the other car, but being in low gear made it impossible.

The other car hit them broadside, crushing the driver's side, flipping Pai's legs one over the other. He cried out in agony. Nadine screamed. Unable to move, he helplessly tried to control his car as it spun around twice before coming to a stop halfway off the precipice of a sheer cliff. Rain poured in through the shattered windshield and drenched his face. He tried to move but excruciating pain shot through his entire body. His first thought was for his son in the crib in the back seat. "Juninho," he whispered, barely able to speak.

Pai could not feel his legs. Juninho! Where was he? He looked to where Nadine was strapped in and her eyes fluttered awake. He moved his head a little and realized where they were. Nadine moaned. "Nadine!" he shouted, trying to wake her up. He could not hear his son. All he heard was the rain.

Nadine moaned and opened her eyes. She instinctually tried to turn around to check on Juninho and could not. "Juninho," she muttered distantly. Her baby was supposed to be there. But he was not. She panicked and tried to turn around again, but the pain was too intense. She gasped when she saw her own arms, blanketed in bruises. Shards of glass were everywhere.

Juninho was nowhere in sight.

Pai felt the tears coming. He muttered a prayer and begged God to take him instead.

"I'm dying," he muttered between gritted teeth. He believed this was the end. Nadine did not respond.

Nadine drifted in and out of consciousness. "Juninho," she said again. The pain was intense.

She realized her husband could not move, so she pushed her shoulder weakly against her door. The frame was twisted and the door was jammed shut, so she couldn't move it. She managed to look out the shattered window. The car dangled over the side of the cliff and the deep canyon far below. She screamed.

"Out the back," Pai said weakly. The car creaked and teetered. Pain shot up both legs. He was afraid if he moved too much, the car would slip off what little roadway it rested on and plummet into the canyon.

"Back window," he struggled to say.

Nadine found she could move in the small crumpled space she was trapped in. She nodded and freed her legs and was finally able to see into the backseat. Juninho's crib was tipped over on the floor, but her son wasn't there. Tears streaked her cheeks. The rear window was completely gone. She scanned the roadway behind her, thinking the unthinkable: that her son was lying somewhere out there on the road.

"Anybody hurt in there?" a strange voice asked. It sounded close.

Pai looked at Nadine. Who said that? He turned and saw a man peering in through Nadine's passenger-side window.

"Can you move?" asked the man.

"No," Pai managed to say.

The man rushed around to the rear of the car, sized up the situation on the cliff side, then returned his attention back to Nadine. "Hurry. Come this way," he beckoned. "I gotta get you out of there."

Nadine nodded and crawled over the front seat into the back and out the rear window.

The car creaked again and knocked some dirt into the canyon. Rocks tumbled downward into the green brushstroke of the river, far below.

The man pulled her to safety, hurried her across the road, and sat her down on the hill on the other side. Then he rushed back across the road to Pai.

"Don't move, sir." the man said. "I've sent my wife back down the hill with my car to call an ambulance."

"My son," Pai managed to whisper.

The man's eyes grew wide. "There is a child in here?!" He scanned the backseat. The crib was upside down and covered in broken glass. He rushed around to the passenger side of the car and pulled the door with all his strength. It did not budge. He gripped the handle again, dug his feet into the dirt, and pulled even harder and the door came open with a loud groan. He dove into the backseat, reached out with both hands through broken glass, and scattered blankets, searching for the boy. He took a deep breath. And when his hands came out from under the backseat, he was holding Juninho, his face streaked with blood. "I found him! And he's alive!"

Pai felt every muscle in his body relax.

The man took his own shirt, wiped away the blood from Juninho's face, and saw the small cut on the boy's forehead above his eyebrow. It looked like an upside-down comma. He pressed down on the cut and after a few moments, the bleeding stopped.

"Take him to his mother," Pai said breathlessly. "Please."

The man looked down at the boy in his arms and Juninho smiled up at him. He smiled back, then hurriedly took him to Nadine.

When Nadine saw her son, she leaped to her feet and grimaced in pain. But that didn't stop her from reaching out and taking her son from the man's arms. "Bless you, bless you," she said over and over, weeping, holding her infant son tightly to her chest.

"God has certainly blessed this little one," the man said. "By the way—he has your smile."

Nadine choked up and smiled as more tears came. "Thank you," she said.

The rain stopped and they heard the distant sound of an approaching ambulance. Nadine closed her eyes, trying to push back the pain.

"I'll stay with you until the ambulance arrives," their savior said and sat down beside her.

Pai heard two things: first, his wife's faint voice talking with the man across the road, then the ambulance siren. He closed his eyes. We are going to be all right, he thought.

The Wizard's Wizard

BRAZILIAN SOCCER is not only a game, it is a way of life, a passion, a constant love for life, the beautiful dance of a nation, a nation that loves to frolic and express itself in the rhythm of the samba and soccer.

The Brazilian national team, known as the Seleção, is the most successful national football team in the history of the FIFA World Cup. They have won five championships: 1958, 1962, 1970, 1994, and 2002. They are also the most successful team in the FIFA Confederations Cup with four titles. Each decade, Brazil introduces their best players to the world and they bring the Brazilian touch and genius to the best clubs in the world. Pelé, the pride of Brazil, is considered the world's best player *ever* to come out of the system. In addition, Brazilian stars such as Garrincha, Zico,

Tostão, Romário, Ronaldo, and many more, made their eternal mark on the world of soccer.

The music and the pleasures of the game flow through Brazil's rivers and the bloodstreams of its people. Soccer in Brazil is not only about efficiency and tactics, it is about joy and beauty. In Brazil, soccer is not only a way of life, it is an art form.

For Pai, like so many Brazilians, playing was like breathing. He yearned to play again, even though his injuries kept him from it for more than a year. In fact, his son, Juninho, who was born on February 5, 1992, walked before he did.

A few months after the accident, out of work with no money to scrape together, Pai moved his family to his parents' house in Nautica 3, a lower-middle class suburb in São Vicente—the same house they were heading for when they had the accident. His father, Ilzemar, was a car mechanic and gave him a job in the garage so they could work together and get Pai back on his feet. Playing soccer was out of the question and Pai knew he had to give up his life's passion for a while. It was more important that he earn a living and support his wife and baby boy.

Neighbors helped them move in. Pai directed traffic from his chair in the biggest room of the house, in which they would live. He instructed his neighbors where to place the furniture.

"The bed goes against the wall, then put the chest of drawers on one end and the armoire on the side and leave some room on the side of the bed to make it a hallway," he told the neighbors. "I'm sorry that I cannot help," he said from his chair in the center of the room. "But I still cannot walk."

One of the neighbors cut him off. "You worry too much, Mr. Neymar," he said. "Mr. Izelmar told me all about it. How you bought him this house with your soccer earnings."

"That's what families are for," Pai said, as he watched his kind neighbors set up the room.

"And this is what neighbors are for," the neighbor said.

It did not take long for the room to be set up and Pai was already playing with his one-year-old son.

"Come to Papa, Juninho!" Pai said, holding out a soccer ball.

Juninho crawled into the room and stopped. He was long and thin with a dark shock of hair, dark skin, and dark piercing eyes. He had a small comma scar above his eyebrow that was barely noticeable. He got it from the piece of flying glass in the accident. When he saw the ball, he crawled swiftly across the floor. When he got to his father, he pulled himself up until he was standing and held out his hands and made a noise that needed no translation: give me the ball! He giggled when his father teased him with it.

Pai held out the ball to his little son. As he looked at Juninho, he thought about how his father, Ilzemar, did not approve of him trying to make a living as a soccer pro. His father always said, "Get a real job first. Play soccer second." But Pai had different plans for Neymar Junior. He was going to encourage Juninho to play the game. Who knows? Maybe he could do what his father could not. It was a worthwhile dream, Pai thought, and he promised himself to do just that.

A couple of months later, Juninho pushed himself up off the ground, wobbled over to his father in his chair, and took the ball from him with a big smile on his face. Then he dropped it and fell back on his rear-end. Everyone laughed, including Grandpa and Grandma, who watched from the front stoop with Nadine.

But when Pai tried to stand to help his son, Nadine shook her finger at him. "Uh-uh, you stay put." She trotted over, lifted Juninho out of the dirt, and brushed him off.

Juninho quickly picked up the ball again.

Pai smiled at his wife and sat back down, wincing from the pain in his healing hip. "How am I going to get back on the field if I can't even stand up?"

"You're not," Nadine said with her usual bluntness and walked back inside with Ilzemar and Grandma.

"That's what you think," he said under his breath as soon as they were out of earshot. He pushed up again, steadied himself, and stood for the first time in hours. Proud of himself, he took a wobbly step and looked down.

Juninho stood in front of him looking up. When he saw his father take a step, he smiled and clapped, dropping the ball again.

Pai laughed. It hurt to laugh, but it didn't matter. He reached behind him, grabbed the chair, pulled it to him, and sat down. He quickly glanced over at the stoop to make sure Nadine or his mother or father hadn't seen him. He held out his hands to his son and Juninho came over and crawled into his lap. "If I can't play ball," Pai said, squeezing his one-year-old son tightly to his chest. "Then I'll teach *you.*"

Some months passed and as Pai slowly healed from his injuries, his son grew and they both got steadier on their feet. One day, Pai stood at one end of the tiny living room using a cane for support and rolled the ball across the floor to his son. Juninho expertly caught it with his foot. "Good!" Pai cheered.

Juninho flashed a smile and his eyes lit up. He kicked it back to his father and his aim was dead on. His father stopped the ball. It hurt a little but every day the pain got a little less. He took his foot off the ball, then golfed it back with his cane. Juninho applauded. "Mine!" he shouted and reached out for his father's walking cane.
He wanted to try it too.

Pai laughed and shook his head. "No, no, no, no! No hands! I can't use my feet yet, that's why I use the cane. You think I *want* to use the cane?" He said, shaking the stick at him. Juninho just giggled at him.

Another day, Juninho stood just outside the back door and tossed his favorite ball in. It rolled into the kitchen, and he had to rush in and grab it before his mama got it.

"Throw that in here one more time, and you're going to eat it for dinner!" she shouted. It worried him. It was his favorite ball. How could he eat it? The idea horrified him, mainly because he had licked it once to see what it tasted like and it tasted awful: like grass, dirt, and whatever else it had rolled around in.

Pai used his walking cane to get across the room to his son. "Let's go outside, Juninho. We're driving Mama nuts playing in here."

Juninho hugged the ball tight to his chest. His father put his hand on his shoulder and helped him out the front door. There was a game to play in the street even if it was just the two of them. There was always a game.

Pai never talked about it much, not even to Nadine, but the most important thing in his life right then was teaching his son the language of soccer. He had a lot to give and he was grateful to God that he had walked away from that accident with his faith intact, even if he couldn't walk for a year. He knew in his heart he would play again, but it would be in God's time, not his, and in the meantime, he would teach his son everything he knew about the beautiful game.

House Ball

"JUNINHO THROWS THE BALL IN!" Juninho shouted
and threw the ball into the room. He was not
only the player, he was also the announcer. The
ball rolled around the bed and down the narrow
hallway, skimming the armoire sideline. He used
his left foot to control it, then expertly shifted it to
his right and dribbled it the length of the bed and
kicked. It sailed past the kitchen and out the back
door. "Goooaaaalllll!" he shouted, hopping up and
down with his arms outstretched, then hammering
his arm. Nadine was in the kitchen, having long
given up on containing her four-year-old son's fury
playing *House Ball.*

Grandma and Grandpa slept in the bedroom and
Pai, Nadine, and Juninho slept in the big room,
partitioned with a family bed, an armoire, and a

chest of drawers that served as walls around the bed. When Rafaella, Juninho's sister, was born, the family bed got crowded and noisy.

Their double bed stood flush against the inside wall of the house. At the foot of the bed, a chest of drawers created a boundary with a narrow hallway between the front of the chest and the foot of the bed. To the side of the bed, an armoire functioned as the other wall of the room with an equal space. This created a hallway that ran from the inside wall along the foot of the bed, turned, went alongside the bed, and ended at the head of the bed: one big L-shaped hallway. For Juninho, it created a space to play. He dribbled the ball from one end of the hallway to the other, then stepped over the ball and shot it back in the opposite direction. Back and forth, within an extremely tight space, he dribbled and created moves of his own and then practiced his moves, over and over, until they were perfect.

"Bicycle kick!" he shouted. He dropped to the shaggy rug and kicked the ball backwards and it landed on the pile of balls on the bed. He leapt in the air dramatically and let the bed catch his fall, scattering his collection of soccer balls in all directions.

"Penalty!" he shouted.

Then he looked up at the twenty or so balls bouncing around the room, some scuffed, some shiny, some large, and some small. He frowned. "Sorry, my friends!" he said and darted about the room collecting them and putting them back on the bed. He held on to one. He never went anywhere without a ball.

Pai worked at his father's auto shop on the outskirts of town. But business was bad because of the economy.

"The shop is slowing down and Dad thinks I should look for more work," he said to Nadine, who sat at the dinner table with Juninho and baby Rafaella.

"I want to help Grandpa too," Juninho said.

"You don't need to work," Pai said, pointing his fork at his son. "You're just a kid. Your job is to play."

Juninho thought about it and smiled. "Yes, sir,"

he said, forking another bite of food.

"What should we do?" Nadine asked her husband.

"One of the customers at the shop—you know, the one with the gummed-up carburetor?" Pai said.

"Oh yeah, that one," Nadine said, teasing him. She had no idea who his customers were.

"Anyway," Pai said. "He said there was an opening at the Traffic Engineering Company in Santos. They need a mechanic. I'm going to apply."

"Fantastic!" Nadine said. "You're a good mechanic. They will be lucky to have you. Does it pay well?"

Pai shrugged. "The same as everything else. Minimum wage. So after I get that job, it won't be enough, so I'll look for another."

Nadine laughed. She was not surprised. There were plenty of jobs in this corner of Brazil, they just didn't pay well. Most people they knew had to hold down three jobs just to pay the bills. And now that they had Rafaella, Neymar Senior had to increase his workload to bring enough food to the table. None of his kids were going to go hungry as long as he was healthy enough to work.

A couple of days later, Pai shook hands with the supervisor at the Traffic Engineering Company in Santos. "We need a mechanic with your expertise," the supervisor said.

"I'm your man," Pai said.

Then the supervisor said a curious thing. "I hear you're a pretty good soccer player."

Pai wondered how he knew, then realized word got around town, particularly when it came to soccer. "I do love the game, sir," Pai said. "I'm no ace, but I was good in my day."

"Good. I need someone to talk to about it," the supervisor said. "You start tomorrow." He started to walk away, then turned back. "By the way, I have two jobs too." Then he smiled and went back inside.

Pai liked him. He stood at the curb and waited for the traffic to die down, then gingerly crossed the street. He had seen a store sign. When he got closer he noticed the note on the door. They were looking for a salesperson. The store was a direct sales outlet for water purifiers.

He walked in and applied for the job. The

owners liked him because by the time he left, he had landed a sales job. He would be going door-to-door, selling Panasonic water filters. It was a good day. He now had three jobs and between them, he hoped would be able to support his family. On his way home, he picked up some strawberries because Nadine loved them. And when he handed them to her and told her he had gotten two new jobs, she kissed him.

House ball was a fun game, but after a while, Juninho got bored playing it alone. He needed some other kids to make it real. He needed goal posts and an opposing team. So he begged his mom to invite his cousins over to play. The minute cousin Jennifer showed up to look after two-year-old Rafaella, Juninho made her a goal post.

His cousins Lorrayne and Rayssa arrived a few minutes later and he made them the opposing team. And since they had no idea how to play, he imagined they were defenders. By virtue of Juninho's soccer expertise, he declared Rafaella old enough to play the other goal post. All three cousins pulled on soccer jerseys of various local clubs. Rafaella drowned in hers because it was four sizes too big. Juninho scanned the teams and the home field and was happy. House ball would never be the same.

The aunts, uncles, and grandparents were out back downing cool fruity summer drinks and chatting and had no idea what was going on inside.

Juninho stepped onto the living room pitch and in his mind, the crowd roared.

Lorrayne and Rayssa giggled, but didn't dare move.

Jennifer stood stock-still and stayed in character as a goal post. Her eyes stared vacantly forward, but deep down inside, she was stifling the laughter that wanted to come out. Rafaella grinned at Jennifer and walked over to her and Jennifer put her back where she belonged as the left-hand goal post.

Juninho dodged across the floor between Lorrayne and Rayssa, and then got behind them and when they ran by, they were tricked into committing a foul.

"Penalty kick!" Juninho shouted and snatched

up the ball. He took his position for the penalty kick by the armoire. He charged the ball, kicked a perfect shot with his left foot, and it sailed between Rafaella, who was busy looking at her shoes, and Jennifer, who had no idea what to do.

"Gooooaaaalllll!" Juninho shouted to the rooftop and pumped his arm.

Pai, Nadine, Pai's brother and his wife, Grandma, and Grandpa all smiled when they heard the kids inside. Juninho loved soccer and was always seen with a soccer ball under his arm. It was not uncommon in Brazil. Millions of other kids did it too.

Pai, who was juggling three jobs, was barely able to support his family, but he knew that his little boy was something special. Maybe, one day, he would fulfill Pai's dream and become a great professional player. In the meantime, they should be grateful for what they had. They were blessed. He saw the smiling faces around him and felt happy.

Another minute passed.

There was another goal, then another. House ball was the best.

Betinho

It was 1998 and Neymar Junior turned six when Pai felt ready to play soccer again. He decided to start by playing *beasal,* a Brazilian offshoot of soccer played on the beach on a small pitch with five players on each team, including the goalkeeper. While playing *beasal* with friends, he was spotted by the manager of Recanto, a local beach team, and after a quick scrimmage where he showed his skills, the manager immediately signed him up on the team.

"You're an ace," the manager said.

"I'm no ace, sir. Maybe, before my accident. But not anymore. Now I fix cars and sell water purifiers," Pai said. "But I love the game. It keeps me sane."

"Well, we wouldn't want you to lose your sanity

and besides, we don't have any other aces down in the basement right now. So you are going to have to be it," the manager countered and stuck out his hand. "The basement" was the nickname of the league.

"Deal?" asked the manager.

Pai flashed a grin and shook his hand. And just like that he was back on a team. It did not pay money, but he was happy.

On the beach near Praia Grande, during a league game, Pai, wearing the Recanto da Vila colors, charged with the ball. A Tumiaru player fouled him, and Pai got ready for a penalty kick. It had been almost six years since the accident and his body was healing but he still felt pain in his hip. He looked okay on the field, but he knew in his heart that his touch wasn't the same.

In the grandstands on the beach, six-year-old Neymar Junior mirrored his father's moves on the pitch, dodging spectators where they sat, including his mother, Nadine, who kept one eye on him and the other on her husband. Her arm was around her two-year-old daughter, Rafaella, sitting next to her.

Luckily, the friendly games Recanto played on the beach usually fell on Nadine's day off from the day care where she worked as a cook, so most games were a family affair. Watching her husband play, Nadine knew he threw his life into every game. So did her son for that matter. Pai would make a move and Juninho would do the exact same thing in the stands. He matched his father's expertise, move-for-move, step for step, and touch for touch. Juninho was a lot quicker, even in the stands. Obstacles weren't annoyances, they were an inspiration to do better.

Down on the beach, Pai took the penalty and missed.

Nadine saw a man watching the game from the beach. At least she *thought* he was watching the game. Because then he did something strange. He turned his back on it! And stared straight at her.

He did not react to the game at all. His eye was on Juninho in the stands, charging down the narrow paths of bench seats, his favorite ball glued to his foot.

The reason the man was even down here was to find his son who came to the beach most days to play a pick-up game before dinner.

The man was broke. He had just turned 40 and he figured the best part of his life was already behind him. He was a star once himself, not for playing ball, but for discovering great players including the Santos and Brazil superstar, Robinho. But that was eight years ago and now he was penniless again. He needed to find another ace before it was too late.

This kid he watched in the stands, he thought, would be perfect on the Futsal team he was forming. He thought the kid was fast. Real fast. Confident. Natural. Full of energy with a superb control of the ball. He was amazed. The boy had so much control in such a confined space, it was uncanny how advanced he was for being so young.

A man jogged past him on the beach and recognized him. "Betinho! What are you doing

here in the basement?" the jogger quipped as he
raced past.

"Looking for my son, my friend!" Betinho
shouted back at the jogger. "And a team, I hope."
he said softly to himself as soon as the jogger
was out of earshot. He took out a handkerchief
and wiped his forehead. It was hot and his sweat
burned his eyes. A moment later, he returned his
attention to the boy in the stands. He looked about
his son's age, the exact age he was looking for
to form a new team. But the game on the beach
hadn't escaped his watchful eye. The kid's father
was quite a good player. His mother was tall and
beautiful. The kid had potential. And great genes.

Nadine watched her husband on the field, when
a shadow fell across her. She looked up and there
was Betinho.

"He has incredible control of the ball," he said,
sitting down beside her.

"He's just getting back on the pitch after a long
recovery from an accident," she answered, absently,
thinking he was talking about her husband. "He

hasn't played in five years, can you believe it?"

"Five years?! But he can't be more than six years old!" Betinho exclaimed.

Nadine looked at the man, confused.

Betinho chuckled and pointed at Juninho who was dribbling the ball this way. "I'm talking about him. I guess he is yours. He looks so much like you. He has your smile."

Nadine burst out laughing. "I thought you were talking about my husband," she said. Then she suddenly looked serious. "I'm sorry, was my son bothering you?"

Betinho smiled. "Not at all," he said and handed her a flyer to read. It called for submissions for a new youth futsal team at Tumiaru he was organizing for Santos FC with boys who were born in 1991 and 1992.

She looked up from the flyer. "Juninho was born in '92!"

"Great!" he said. "Bring him this week. I want to see him on the field. If he's half as good on the pitch as he is in the stands, we want him," he

continued. "I hope you don't think me rude, but—
where on Earth did he learn those moves?"

"House ball," Nadine said, matter-of-factly.
Earlier that day, Juninho had sent his favorite ball of
the day sailing into the floor lamp that stood in for a
right goal post, knocking it over, breaking the bulb,
and smashing the shade. That was the dark side of
house ball.

"House ball?" Betinho laughed. "Well, whatever
that is—he is talented."

"Talented?" Nadine asked. "Really? I will talk
to his father." Then she smiled. "I'm sure he will
agree." She went back to watching Pai play and
enjoying himself. She looked forward to telling him
the good news.

The First Team

JUNINHO HELD ON to his father as he downshifted
the motorcycle and took the turn at a forty-five
degree angle. Although he went everywhere with
his dad on his motorbike, he could never get over
the sharp turns and the speed. The g-force pushed
Juninho down into the leather seat and he squeezed
his eyes shut, praying he wouldn't fall off. Neymar
Senior turned the motorbike in the opposite direction
and spun into the small dirt lot beside the Baixada
Santista gymnasium where Clube Tumiaru had an
indoor court, skidding to a stop in the loose gravel.
He swiftly got off, lifted his son, and set him down
on the ground. Juninho's knees shook, but he hid it.
He wouldn't want his father to think he was scared.

They were always talking about the game. Father
and son. Pai explained to Juninho about creativity.

He talked about how players create their own style of play. There is a spark that great players have in them that lift them above all the others and makes them special. He knew that Juninho might not understand what he was talking about because he was still so young. But he also knew that creativity had to start early. And it had to begin with trust. Juninho never tired of hearing his dad talk about soccer.

"It's called improvisation," Pai said as he ushered his son into the gym. "Do you know what that means?" His voice echoed off the gymnasium walls.

"No," Juninho said. He was wearing a plain t-shirt. He said it again because he wanted to hear his echo.

"It is the soul of a great player," his father replied. "Improvisação," he repeated, this time emphasizing the syllables. "Mind to foot," he said pointing to his head and then to his foot. "You do something—like a stepover—but you do it your way."

"Like when I play in the house?" Juninho asked.

"Exactly. You don't think about it ahead of time.

There is no time for that out there on the pitch. Or here, on the Tumiaru futsal court. It is all mind to foot. *Heart* to foot, really."

Juninho studied his father and nodded. To him, he was the greatest man in the world. And he was a pro and he had taught him so much about the beautiful game. Everything he knew about soccer, he learned from his father and his grandfather. Just like everything he learned about the heart, he learned from his mother.

"Invent something out there and if it works, practice it until you get it perfect."

"With this one?" Juninho asked sticking out his right foot. "Or this one?" He stuck out his left foot.

"Either foot. Get great with both and you will always have a better chance of winning," said Pai.

Juninho grinned and wrinkled up his nose.

Pai smiled back. God, he was proud of his son! And when the boy smiled like that and wrinkled up his nose and his forehead, he could see the thin scar from the accident coming out of his eyebrow like an upside down comma. No one noticed it but him.

You had to know where to look. The smile, then, always reminded him of the accident: how he felt when he was afraid they had lost him. It reminded him what a gift their son was to them.

"Ready?" he asked, taking his son by the shoulders.

Juninho hugged his father. "House ball! Only bigger." He trotted out on the small wooden futsal floor where Betinho and the other players were waiting for him.

A few minutes later, Betinho watched with amazement as Juninho tore up the Tumiaru *futsal* court. Like *beasal,* futsal is played on a smaller pitch, mainly indoors. The name comes from the Portuguese *futebol de salão,* which means "hall football." It was developed in Brazil and Uruguay in the 1930s and 1940s. There are five players on each team including the keeper, and the ball is smaller. It's a great way to develop a player's individual skills and team play.

When the scrimmage began, the other players never knew what hit them. Juninho was fast and confident and he never seemed to tire. It took

Betinho a few minutes to remind himself that his instincts when he first saw the boy on the beach were spot on. The kid was spectacular. "I think we have found our ace," Betinho said to himself and cornered Juninho as he came off the court. "First of all, I want you to know you are on the team."

Juninho bounced around with joy as his dad came over. Betinho stuck his hand out and they shook. "He's great," he said.

Pai chuckled. "I was just about to ask you what you thought."

Betinho turned to Juninho: "Where did you *learn* those tricks?"

"In my house," Juninho said and Pai and Betinho both laughed.

"He's not kidding," Pai said.

"Well, I was impressed when I first saw him in the stands," Betinho retorted. "I can only imagine that his house work is even better!" Both men laughed although Juninho had no idea why.

Betinho marveled at the boy. Learning to control the ball in tight spaces was what soccer was all about. This was better than he expected. Pai returned to the stands to watch his son play. He took notes so he could work with Juninho later.

The Baixada Santista indoor Futsal court was where the entry-level Santos teams played. The boys who shone here would eventually make it to the grass pitch. Pai knew it was a good start. He leaned into Betinho's ear and whispered, "I have to get back to work."

"Oh, of course! How rude of me, I did not even ask. What do you do, Mr. Silva Santos?" Betinho asked.

"I fix cars and sell water purifiers," Pai answered. "Actually, I have three jobs. Money is tight, you know..."

Betinho knew right away the family was struggling. "Well, we are going to try to make things better for you. I can offer you enough food stamps per month to feed your whole family. How does that sound?"

It sounded great to Pai. They badly needed the help. He had three jobs and he still wasn't making ends meet. Having his food taken care of was huge and Betinho's offer moved him. But he was a tough ball player. So he smiled and just said, "Thank you, Betinho. It's a good start."

Scoring Left and Right

Jardim Glória was off the bay island shared by Santos and São Vicente, near the shore. It was a poor neighborhood with drab shanties. Drab until the da Silva Santos family moved into the bright green house that Pai built. It was the first real color in the neighborhood in a long time.

Some months after the family had settled in, Betinho pulled up in his car, set his parking brake, and got out. He saw the boys playing pick-up in the street. They were a little ways up the hill. He smoothed his shirt and then marched up towards them. He saw Juninho first, in the middle of the road, running up the street with the ball glued to his feet. Betinho cleared his throat and all the guys stopped playing. "You're late!" he said. "There's a game today!" The other boys knew that when there was practice or a game, they had to stop the pick-up until Juninho could get back.

Juninho, wearing his blue and white Tumiaru number 7 jersey, walked over with a broad grin on his face. Once he joined Betinho, they both went back down the hill. He happily climbed into Betinho's rickety old car and the two of them sped off for the salão.

Over the past months, Juninho earned the number 7 jersey. Everyone in the organization had no doubt he was brilliant—everyone but Juninho. If you asked him, he wouldn't know what you were talking about. For him, it was what he did every day—play the way his father and grandfather and Betinho taught him: all out. Whether it was in the house, in the streets, in the stands, or on the court, it did not matter. The only thing that mattered was that his head and his heart were in it to win it.

On the Futsal court at Baixada Santista, he loved the sound of his shoes hitting the floor in the gymnasium. He knew exactly how many steps it took him to get from one end to the other. Knowing that, he could gauge where all his teammates were by the number of steps they were from him at any given time. He loved to double pass with his pal Dudu, a happy kid with dark curly hair.

At half time, Betinho signaled to Juninho and he trotted over. "Use your right foot," he said.

"I do," Neymar replied.

"Only your right foot," Betinho insisted.

Juninho looked at him, confused. "Really?" He thought about it for a moment, then shrugged. "Okay," he said.

When the half-time break was over, he hurried out to his position and the game resumed. But the more he thought about it, the more confused he got. His father always taught him to use *both* feet. Then again, Betinho was the boss. What was he supposed to do?

Dudu asked him, "What did Betinho tell you?"

"To use my right foot."

"What *else* is new?" Dudu said.

"But I like to use *both*."

"Of course you do. That is why you are well-rounded," Dudu said. "But not in math!"

Juninho felt his face blush and he stopped in
his tracks. Dudu was in his class at school and
always wound up helping him with his math. It
was frustrating, Juninho thought. He could figure
out where everyone was on the field—but he just
didn't get all those problems that the teacher wrote
on the blackboard. The thought of just how lousy
he was at math kept his mind occupied for a split
second and that was just long enough for the ball to
shoot right past him.

Luckily, Dudu was there, seized it, and stabbed
it right back to him. "Pay attention!" he shouted,
pointing at him and laughing all the way down the
court.

Juninho laughed too. His father's rule came
to mind. "Rule 62," he would say. "Don't take
yourself so serious."

Juninho took the ball, weaved down the court,
and slammed it into the left corner of the net,
fooling the goalkeeper. Pai, who had taken a break
from work to watch his son play, leaped to his feet

and cheered, then realized he was the only one standing, except for Betinho. The other parents were busy talking and did not even acknowledge his son's goal. A minute later one of their kids got the ball and the parents were all on their feet.

So that's how it is, Pai thought.

Out on the court, Juninho got the ball again and within seconds, had a perfect shot at the goal.

"Left foot! Left foot!" Pai shouted from the sidelines, bouncing around excitedly.

Juninho had a better shot with his left foot, but, remembering the orders from his coach, flipped it to the right and took his shot. The ball sailed straight, right over the net and into the crowd.

"Some ace," one of the fathers spat at Betinho.

Betinho smiled politely, then ignored him. He was used to parents fighting for their kids. Juninho was disappointed with his shot. Why bother with the right foot if you have a perfectly good touch with the left?

Out on the sidelines, Pai was thinking the same thing. They had practiced that move together.

Why *didn't* he use his left foot? He got up and went over to Betinho. "He should have used his left foot," Pai said.

Betinho never took his eyes off the court. "He didn't because I told him not to," he said.

Pai riveted him with a glare. "I beg your pardon?"

"I told him to only use his right foot. It's his strong foot. Old school. That's how I've always done it."

Pai smiled, but it was one of his special smiles. The kind Nadine characterized as a smile you don't want to get on the other side of.

"I'm sorry, but that is not going to work for us," Pai said.

"Mister da Silva, I don't think you—"

"Stop," Pai interrupted. "Never get between me and my son. I have always taught him and trained him to use both feet," he said. "He is that good. If I were you, I would rethink that training method. It may be old school to you—but to me, it's just old."

With that, Pai walked away and took up a position down near the court, closer to Juninho and farther from Betinho. The next time the ball went out, he beckoned his son over and whispered something in his ear. Juninho shot a quick look to Betinho, in his seat, then back to his dad, and nodded, then went back out on the court.

Betinho scratched his head. Life is too short, he thought. Besides, Pai was probably right. "I just can't win today," he muttered to himself, then slumped down in his seat. The father of another player sitting nearby looked like he was about to say something and Betinho held up his hand and silenced him. "I'll move your boy forward when he plays like that," he said, pointing to the court, where Juninho dribbled the ball and nutmegged it to Dudu at the other touchline. Dudu ticked it back and Juninho sunk it like a surgeon.

The next day after school, the boys played pickup in the street. Betinho drove up. He got out and walked up the hill toward the boys. "Let's go, Juninho!" he shouted.

In reply, the boys shouted at him and wildly waved their arms.

Betinho, amused, waved his arms wildly back.

"Hurry up!"

Juninho pointed and shouted, "Betinho! Your car!"

Betinho spun around just in time to see his car, rolling down the hill backwards! He had forgotten to set the parking brake. He stood there, stunned, for a long time, not knowing what to do. The car rolled down the hill, faster and faster, heading straight for a busy intersection.

Juninho and the boys charged downhill after Betinho's car. Juninho passed the rest as if they were standing still and ran so fast he finally caught up with the car. The window was open so he sped up and timed his dive perfectly in through the window and landed on the front seat of the speeding car.

"Parking brake!" Betinho shouted breathlessly from up the street

The car entered the intersection backwards.

Juninho found the hand brake in between the seats and yanked up. There was a loud grinding and the car skidded and fishtailed to a stop in the middle of the intersection. Horns blared as cars careened around them.

Betinho caught up and quickly yanked the door open. He saw Neymar Junior sitting behind the wheel with a mischievous smile on his face.

"Great run, huh, Coach?" he asked.

"No one can catch you," Betinho said, breathless.

"What about my dive, Coach?" Juninho insisted.

"Amazing," said Betinho

Juninho moved to the other seat and Betinho climbed behind the wheel. The rest of the boys ran up and piled in. Betinho started the engine and headed back up the hill. When he pulled over at the top in front of Juninho's house, he finally caught his breath. His heart raced. He looked around at the boys. They weren't the least bit tired. 'Well,' he thought. 'At least they got a good workout.' He started laughing and the laughter was infectious and soon all of them were laughing uproariously. He was relieved. That was a close one.

"And what did we learn today, Betinho?" Juninho asked.

"That you should be ready when I get here?"

Betinho asked.

"NO!" the boys all shouted.

"That you should set your parking brake!" Juninho said.

Betinho laughed. The kid was right.

The other boys piled out of the car. "See you tomorrow, Betinho!"

"That was fun!"

"Let's do it again!"

Betinho laughed and drove away with Juninho.

Juninho waved to his friends from the car and they waved back as Betinho aimed the car toward the club.

Sleeping Beauty

JUNINHO WATCHED his dad push a seed spreader
back and forth up one side of the backyard and
down the other. The ground had been marked off
in a large rectangle about the same size as a futsal
court. Pai hammered short wooden stakes into the
ground and strung kite string between them to
keep everyone from walking on the seeded ground.
Juninho watched intently with his baby sister
Rafaella at his side. "Garden," Rafaella said.

"No," Juninho said. "Something better."

Rafaella clapped.

The whole thing turned green in a week. "It's
a futsal court!" Juninho said, watching his father
water the sprouting court. "With grass."

"Lucky guess," Pai joked and kept watering.

Juninho thought it was the best thing that had

happened to him. A pitch in their own backyard! The long grassy rectangle fit perfectly. It was no bigger or no smaller than the indoor salão at Clube Tumiaru. But it was softer. And greener. Pai admired his handiwork. He provided the backbreaking labor and Betinho brought the grass seed. It was a good idea to keep the neighborhood kids off the street and give Juninho a great place to practice.

One day, while his parents were at work, Juninho invited his friends over for their first pick-up game in his backyard. Much to his surprise, 20 kids showed up. They loved the new pitch and everyone wanted to try it out.

They played until the sun hit the ocean with a flash of green. Six hours, non-stop. It was a neighborhood record. It was only then that Juninho noticed there was no more grass left. Just the sandy soil that had been there before Pai planted the grass. It looked like the beach. They had destroyed the pitch in one day. "When my dad gets home, I'm gonna get it!" he wailed, freaked out. "What am I going to do?

"Tell him the truth," one boy said.

"Act surprised," said another.

"Go to bed early," said a third boy.

"Wait, what?" Juninho stopped. "What did you say?"

"Whenever I don't want my mom or dad to find out about something," the boy explained. "I go to bed early. If I'm asleep, they're not gonna wake me up, right? I sleep until they go to work and I don't have to talk about it. Eventually they forget," the kid shrugged.

Juninho had to admit, it was beautiful in its simplicity. But he agonized over it. Mom and Dad always taught him to tell the truth. But, no grass—and the truth might get him grounded.

The guys scattered in all directions and headed to their homes in Jardim Glória, and Juninho waited at the kitchen door for his mom. He yawned when Nadine entered.

She went straight to the kitchen and started preparing supper.

He stretched.

"Wash your hands, supper will be ready soon,"

Nadine said.

He yawned again.

Nadine gave him a look. "You feeling okay?" she asked.

He yawned again. And stretched. "Tired. I-I think I'm gonna go to bed now," he said and walked into the next room.

Nadine was puzzled, but not suspicious. "But your father isn't home yet," she said, pouring some noodles into the boiling water.

"Yeah, I know," he shouted from the next room. "What about dinner?"

Juninho sat on the side of his bed and realized he had forgotten all about supper when he had devised his plan. And he was starving. He decided it would be better if he ate, then went to bed. He marched back into the kitchen and sat down at his usual place at the table. Nadine spooned some gravy over a plate of noodles for him. Rafaella sat in her wooden high chair across from him.

"You can always sleep after you eat," Nadine said and served herself. "If you're really that tired."

"Thanks, Mom," Juninho said, "I really am. Then he gave her one last fake yawn, before he started shoveling the noodles into his mouth and eating ravenously. Six straight hours of playing ball and he was running on empty. It took him less than three minutes to finish dinner and he was fast asleep a few minutes after that.

But when his father came home, he woke up. He could hear them talking softly in the kitchen.

"He's asleep," Nadine said when Pai walked in. It was already dark. "Don't wake him," she said.

Juninho smiled from his bed, then had a realization: if his father looked out in the backyard he might see that there was no grass. How could he miss it? Maybe this was not such a good idea after all. He groaned. Maybe he didn't look. After all, it was dark out.

Pai discovered the destruction of the grass on the backyard pitch the minute he came home, and so, during that week while his son avoided him by sleeping, he replanted the grass. It grew back in a couple of days and one morning he got tired of waiting for his son to catch on, so he decided to stay home a little while longer. When Juninho came into the kitchen, ready for school, he was shocked to find his father waiting for him at the breakfast table. "Sleeping beauty!" he said cheerfully and sipped his coffee. "I almost didn't recognize you."

Juninho thought he was going to barf he was so wracked with guilt. He did not know what to say. His heart raced. He nervously sat down across from his father. He wanted to get off the planet. What had he done?! He was a dead duck!

"I was worried maybe you got the sleeping sickness," Pai joked.

Juninho saw that more grass had been planted and the seeds were starting to sprout, but he couldn't muster up the courage to confess to his father. Finally he could not hold it in anymore. "Dad, I-, I'm the one who ruined the pitch."

Pai raised an eyebrow, shot his wife a look, and then nodded seriously. "I think we should talk. Before Betinho gets here," he said, then finished his morning coffee.

Face to Face with God

"DAD," JUNINHO SAID, sitting at the breakfast table. "You know how you always taught me to tell you if I did something wrong?" he asked.

"Of course. What would life be like if we did not admit when we were wrong?" Pai said.

"I-, I was hiding from you because I was afraid you would be mad that we ruined the pitch," Juninho confessed. He looked his father in the eye.

"Hiding? Like an ostrich? Did you really think I wouldn't notice?" Pai exclaimed.

"How did you know?" Juninho asked, knowing for sure his plot had been foiled.

"Oh, I don't know, let's see. I came home from work and the pitch was pounded to sand. Evidently, someone had *played* on it! So I planted some more grass seed the next day. *You* didn't notice because you had your head stuck in the sand. Take a look. It's coming in nicely."

Juninho got up and looked out back. He came back to the table, his face red with embarrassment. "Are you mad at me?" he asked.

"Mad? No. I am happy," Pai replied and chuckled.

"Happy?" Juninho said. Grown-ups were totally confusing.

"Sure. I built you that pitch to *play* on—and you played on it until it was nothing but sand. What do you think a pitch is for?"

"But we wrecked it."

"You wrecked it *playing* on it. You did exactly what you were *supposed* to do," his father said. "Don't worry—just play," he said.

They heard the unmistakable rattling of Betinho's car as it struggled to turn off. Chug chug chug cough!

Betinho stuck his head in the door and saw they had been talking. He came to take Juninho to school. He did this as a favor to Pai, whenever he had to leave early for work, so he was surprised to see them all still at home.

"Oh, I see sleeping beauty finally woke up!" he said.

"I did!" Juninho said. "Did you see the backyard? The grass is growing back!"

Betinho grinned at Pai and Nadine, and then turned his attention to his soccer student. "Will you look at that?" he said and winked at Pai. "Amazing how that works." He draped his arm over Juninho's shoulder, guided him toward the door, and as they passed the table, he snatched up a piece of toast. "For the road," he said to Nadine and then they were gone.

Later that week, on a Thursday, Pai decided the family needed to find a church.

Juninho remembered a big blue one in São Vicente with the words "Face to Face with God" painted on the front. Everyone agreed that it sounded like the right church for them so Juninho and his father paid it a visit.

The Peniel Baptist Church was presided over by Pastor Newton Lobato, a husky man with graying hair, piercing brown eyes, and an engaging smile that drew you in. When he gave his fiery sermon that day, his powerful voice boomed through the worship hall. There were a thousand people crammed into the building to hear the Pastor and way in the back, Juninho leaned against the chair in front of him and listened intently to his every word. Later, he prayed privately with Lobato and the pastor told him his congregation met every Thursday and to come back.

A couple of years later, father and son began a tradition that would stay with them forever. They would either recite a Bible verse together before Juninho took the field, or Pai would shove a piece of paper in his son's hand containing a verse from Isaiah:

Fear not, for I am with you: be not dismayed for I am your God.

Gremetal

BETINHO KNOCKED ON THE DOOR of Juninho's house. It was 2001 and his star pupil was nine years old. He had news for the whole family.

Nadine answered the door. "Come in," she said, ushering him into the living room. "Have you eaten?"

"I'm fine," Betinho said. "Better than fine," he said, patting his stomach. "Is Pai here?" A minute later, Pai showed Betinho out to the backyard where they could talk.

Juninho and Nadine watched through the window in the kitchen wondering what was so important.

The two men sat down on the grassy pitch and relaxed as cotton-ball clouds drifted slowly by on their way inland from the sea.

"I have taken a coaching position at Portuguesa Santista," Betinho announced.

Portuguesa Santista was the Associação Atlética Portuguesa, also known as Briosa. It was the Santos soccer team that was founded by the Portuguese population of São Paulo in 1917.

"Don't tell me you are here to move Juninho to Briosa?! He's too young!" Pai said.

"Okay, I won't tell you that," Betinho teased.

"Good. You had me worried."

"No, I'm not going to move him to Briosa," Betinho said. "I want to bring him to Gremetal. They have a good futsal team and training program. It can be a *great* futsal team," he said. "With Juninho." Betinho was talking about the *Escolinha de Futsal* at Gremetal, a sporting organization in São Paulo started by a bunch of Brazilian scientists who loved soccer and wanted to get the kids off the streets.

"Will they take him?" Pai asked.

Betinho smiled. He had been planning this for ages. "They already said yes. I'll be taking a bunch of kids over to Gremetal. If Juninho does well, then it's Briosa, and one day, who knows, one day we might see him play at Santos."

Santos FC was the legendary city club, one of the best clubs in Brazil. Everyone called them *The Fish*. In the past, their opponents would mock them by chanting that they were *fishmongers*. The Santos FC players turned the insult around and nicknamed themselves *The Fish*. The name stuck. Santos was the most successful club in the Brasileirão League. They were national champions eight times, a distinction only achieved by Palmeiras.

"Of course, we need to take baby steps," Betinho said. "Gremetal is the first step."

"Aren't the boys older at Gremetal?" Pai asked.

"So what? He can cope with them. As a matter of fact, he will do great," Betinho said.

"Who will do great?" Juninho asked, coming out of the house and joining them on the grass.

"You," Betinho said. "We are talking about Gremetal. Heard of it?"

"Sure," Juninho said. "It's a futsal team."

"It's going to be your futsal team," Betinho said. "If you want it."

Juninho stopped in his tracks. "It sounds fantastic!" he said, then stopped as a worried look crept over his face. "But what about my friends?"

"Dudu will be there," Betinho said.

"Awesome!" Juninho said and started running around the backyard pitch, dribbling a ball.

"The plan," Betinho said, turning to Pai. "Is to move 10 or 11 of my best players there. Coaching Portuguesa Santista gives me a say in who goes and who gets accepted to Gremetal," Betinho explained. "And when he's ready, I'll have a place for him at Briosa."

Juninho skidded to a stop next to the men. "Am I really going?"

"Yes, Juninho, we are going to make some noise. Win some awards," Betinho said. "You will be on the first Under-11 team ever at Gremetal.

"It will be the best futsal team in Santos!" his dad said. He looked happy.

"So it is decided?" asked Betinho.

"Agreed," Pai said, shaking Betinho's hand.

"And you make sure I stay on as coach," Betinho

added, flashing a smile, then a shrug. "We don't want to change in midstream."

Pai grinned. "You are too smart for me, Betinho," he said. "Of course! No Betinho? No Juninho."

Betinho was pleased and hugged Pai. "By the way," he said. "I want to thank you."

"For what?" Pai asked.

"I took your advice. About letting the boys play with both feet."

Pai hugged his friend. "Thanks for telling me. It must be really hard for an old dog to learn new tricks." he smiled.

"Extremely," Betinho said.

The next day, Betinho took the coaching position at Portuguesa Santista and brought a whole bunch of boys to Gremetal.

Juninho looked up at the Gremetal building. He couldn't believe he was really here. He knew soccer was fun, he just didn't expect it to keep getting better and better. He loved to play the game most Brazilians loved and because of his love and passion for it, he was just better at it. He earned his place in the game by playing well, but it was more than that, at least in Betinho's mind. Betinho believed that Juninho had the potential to one day bring back the free spirit creativity that he believed was missing from Brazilian soccer for the past few years. He talked about it many times and Pai would just nod in agreement.

Juninho didn't move a muscle. He just stared up at the front of Gremetal in awe.

"What are you waiting for?" Betinho asked. "Let's go in."

Minutes later, Juninho, wearing the number 14 yellow shirt with the green collar of Gremetal, darted from one end of the court to the other, the ball glued to his foot, and with two defenders blocking him, lobbed the ball straight at them. At the last moment, the ball dropped like a leaf and rolled into the net.

Alcides Junior Magri, the Gremetal coach, turned to Betinho, amazed. "Nine years old and he's doing a falling leaf like he's been doing it for years!"

"Trust me, Junior," Betinho said proudly. "He has been doing it for years. He was born with this game fully formed in his psyche."

"Whatever that means," Magri said. "What else can I do to help?"

"Warn me." Betinho replied and Magri looked instantly confused. "Warn me before you move him up to the Under 13s."

Coach Magri laughed and slapped his old friend's back. "You read my mind."

And in that moment, Juninho scored another goal.

On the ride home, Juninho could not stop talking. He loved his new teammates and he was excited to get into some real contests with real teams in real games.

Candle Night

"GET THE CANDLES!" shouted Pai as he and Juninho charged out of the kitchen and into the darkened house. They had just sat down to dinner when the lights went out. As soon as the house went pitch dark, no one paid attention to the food on the table.

Nadine could not move. She froze in her chair. She was afraid this was going to happen.

Juninho rushed back in with two fat candles and set them on the table. Pai came in a moment later with some more candles and lit them all. Soon the kitchen flickered in candlelight. The windows were open and crickets chirped loudly outside as Juninho and Pai's shadows cast waving chevrons and imaginary goblins across the backyard soccer pitch.

"There! That's better," Pai proudly announced, glancing over at Nadine.

Nadine scowled at him. 'How could that be *better?* she thought. But she held her tongue. Jobs were hard to find and money was scarce, even with her helping the finances working at the daycare center. Four jobs between them and they still couldn't keep the lights on. They hadn't paid the electric bill and the company turned out the lights. It depressed her. She pretended to be okay but she was not and Pai knew it.

"This is fantastic!" Juninho shouted and Rafaella giggled. She pushed away from the table, danced in front of the candles with Juninho, and pointed at their shadows that stretched across the backyard pitch like gigantic shadow puppets.

Nadine looked across the table at her husband and smiled. "It's not your fault," she said. Pai reached across the table, took her hand, and held it tight.

"I'll fix this, don't worry," he said, but in his mind it was not only depressing, but also humiliating.

She knew they were in this together and when he took her hand, she felt better. She wanted to smile, but she just wasn't ready. At least, not yet. But the children's dancing was hard to ignore. They were happy with the candles and turned the whole thing into a fun game; and the fun was infectious.

Juninho and Rafaella each took their parents' hands, pulled them up, and danced with them. No music was playing but Juninho could hear it in his head. The same joyful rhythm he heard whenever he played the beautiful game. The candles flickered in the wind they made in the tiny room and their shadows danced wildly around, splashing through the windows and beyond.

Pai moved closer to Nadine and put his arm around her. She rested her head on his shoulder and they watched their children make the best of a bad situation. "And to think I thought this was the worst day of my life," Nadine said as she snuggled up to her husband.

Pai smiled. "You have to admit—it is kind of fun," he replied.

A little later Pai walked Juninho off to bed, carrying Rafaella who had already fallen fast asleep.

He tucked her in then went over to Juninho's bed and tucked him in.

"Dad?"

"Yes, son?" Pai replied.

"Someday I'm gonna build a place in Praia, just for kids to play. And the lights will never go out."

"That's a very good thought, son," Pai said.

"Dad?"

"Mm?"

"I love soccer."

"I know you do. I love it too. Do you want to hear the soccer story again?"

"Yes!" Juninho's eyes shone with excitement.

"Years ago," Pai began, "before we had to adapt our game to play like the Europeans and the rest of the world, we played a kind of ball that only Brazilians knew. Pelé knew it. And Garrincha and Zico and Didi, and many more. It was how the Seleção, our national team, played. And they won magnificently. But when we had to compete with Europe, we began to change our style and some of it was lost. Do you remember what we called it?"

"Ginga!" Juninho said instantly. He had heard this story a hundred times from his dad but he never tired of it. Ginga was the basis of *Capoeira,* a Brazilian martial art that mixed dance with acrobatics and music with combat. Legend was, it was brought to Brazil by African slaves as a game. It was really a combat technique and in the rain forest the slaves disguised the fight as a dance to keep themselves from being executed by their masters. When soccer came to Brazil, the people instilled it in their Capoeira heritage. It is a style of play unlike any in any other country in the world.

"Yes, Ginga," Pai said. "The Seleção does not play this way anymore. But we should not forget it, son."

"I won't, dad. It is what you taught me," Juninho said.

"I showed you, but I did not teach you. It is in our blood. And you must be ready when it is your turn to play for the Seleção."

Juninho reached out, wrapped his arms around his father's neck, and squeezed him tight. "I'll be ready," he said softly.

"Look at me," Pai said and his son obeyed. "Mark my words. One day you *will* play for the Seleção."

Juninho was excited at the thought and the scar on his forehead became more visible.

It served as a reminder to Pai that Juninho was a gift. He held back the tears. A shadow fell across him. He looked over at the doorway and there was Nadine standing there, listening. She came over and reached out her hand and Pai took it and she helped him to his feet. They both walked back to their room.

In the morning, Pai and Nadine were relieved they did not have to rely on candlelight during the day; the sun took care of that. Juninho and Rafaella, on the other hand, could not wait for night to come, so their candle night adventure could begin again.

Neymar Jr.

JUNINHO AND HIS FAMILY lived without lights for a
week before the electric company finally turned
them back on, thanks to Gremetal, who paid
the bills. Pai was eternally grateful to them, but
they would have none of his thanks. They felt
it was their duty because it was their mission as
an organization. The well-being of the children
and their families always came first. Juninho was
special to them. The boy played wonderfully. Over
the next few months, every ball Juninho touched
turned to gold and Gremetal won every tournament
they entered. Juninho was just eleven when they
moved him up to the Under 13 team.

"Juninho can't be ours forever," Coach Alcides
explained to Betinho, although Betinho needed
no explanation. It was obvious why they needed

Juninho on the older team: he was great. "With him playing on the U13s, we have a shot at winning some titles before he leaves."

"A shot?" Betinho laughed. "You'll win it!"

Juninho felt right at home on the new team. Léo Dentinho, a kid he knew well, was on the team. From the moment they both stepped out on the court, they became best friends and enjoyed playing together. Juninho and Leo practiced three days a week. What Léo Dentinho did not know, Juninho passed on to him. They complemented each other.

Lunch was always at noon at Gremetal and as soon as Alcides blew the whistle all the boys charged off the court and raced each other to the canteen for their midday meal.

"Go to the canteen!" Coach Alcides shouted at Juninho and Leo.

"No thanks, Coach," Juninho shouted back. "We're going to practice."

They continued practicing, then later ate leftover sandwiches from the boys who went to lunch.

Playing with the older boys made Juninho much better. And, as Betinho predicted, the move paid off.

At the final against Santos, Juninho was on the left. Leo, on the right, shot the ball across the court to him. He did a brilliant pass back to his partner, and Leo sunk the ball into the left side of the net. A few minutes later, Leo got the ball and shot another bullet across the court to Juninho who shot it back as they moved up the court and one more time, Leo, wearing number 10, was there to intercept and arc the ball into the net. Then, in the final minutes of the futsal match, Juninho and Leo did another double pass and when the ball came back to Juninho, he passed the defender in front of him and sunk the ball into the net, scoring the final goal. They won their first title ever, *The Copa Uniligas,* 3–1.

Fino, the head coach at Portuguesa Santista— also known as Briosa—was watching the game. His team was one of the lower division teams in Santos and their youth team was perfect for Juninho. When the referee blew the whistle, Fino approached Betinho.

"I want him on my team," he said.

"Let me talk to his parents," Betinho replied. He knew it was coming and smiled. Everything was working out exactly as he had planned.

They drove in Betinho's car straight up *Avenida Ana Costa* from the sea, then cut over *Rua Joaquim Tavora* to *Avenida Senador Pinheiro Machado* and turned into the dirt parking lot that bordered the modest *Ulrico Mursa Stadium* and the *Portuguesa Santista* grounds. A few minutes later Juninho stood and stared at the stadium that held 10,000 people. In his eyes it looked huge and beautiful. It had real grass and the pitch and the stands looked magnificent. He yearned to play on it.

"What do you think?" Betinho asked. He was holding a shopping bag. Juninho tried to peer inside it, but Betinho wouldn't let him.

"It's amazing," Juninho finally said. He had been here before, with his father, but only as a spectator.

Beyond the buildings, there was a futsal court

where Juninho would play, another smaller field, and a swimming pool. Even if he had to wait until he was twelve to get off the futsal court—it wasn't that far off.

"How far are we from Urbano Caldeira?" he asked.

Betinho burst out laughing. The kid was just about to play here and he had already set his sights on the big stadium up the street, he thought. "Two blocks," he said. "And don't worry, Juninho. You'll get there." Urbano Caldeira was the stadium and home of The Fish, the Santos Futebol Clube.

Juninho shrugged. "I've already been. With my father."

"So Pelé must be your hero then, huh?" Betinho asked.

"He's okay," Juninho hesitated.

Betinho laughed. Pelé, the king of soccer, the symbol of Brazilian soccer, was the best ever and Santos' all-time top goal scorer and appearance holder. And Juninho thinks he's just okay?

"I have other heroes." Juninho shrugged.

"Okay, but what about teams? Santos is still

your favorite team, right?"

Juninho shook his head. "Palmeiras," he said
with a grin.

Betinho was shocked. "What?!"

Juninho shrugged. "You asked."

"Of course, you know this is heresy—but I
promise I won't tell anyone your favorite team is
Palmeiras!" Betinho said.

This time Juninho laughed. "You better not!"
Where they came from, you had to be a Santos fan.
"What about Ronaldo?" Betinho asked, amused.
Ronaldo Luís Nazário de Lima, nicknamed The
Phenomenon, was the biggest Brazilian star of his
time, an amazing striker who just recently led the
Brazilian tem to win the 2002 World Cup

"He is the best," Juninho said. "One day I'd like
to win a World Cup like him."

"That's what I like to hear," Betinho said. "Here,
you've been dying to see what I have in this bag,"
he said. He opened the bag, fished around in it, and
pulled out a pure white Portuguesa Santista jersey
with *Neymar Jr.* on the back and the number 10.

Juninho couldn't believe it. He took his shirt off and pulled on the new jersey. It fit perfectly and he proudly puffed out his chest. "I love it! Thank you!"

Betinho loved Juninho like his own son and hugged him. He could not think of another kid he knew who loved the game as much as Juninho. "You earned it."

A year later, in 2004, when Juninho was 12, a television crew set up their cameras and lights in the Briosa futsal court, preparing to televise the State Championship. Although no one knew who Neymar Jr. was, he showed up with a new haircut: cut close to the scalp with a thick black smudge of hair up front, like a cocked hat.

By the time the match was over, all cameras were on Juninho. The crowd shouted "NEYYY-MMARRRRRRRRRRRRRR!" as he cut between a wall of defenders and blasted a shot at the goalkeeper, who did not see it coming.

The fans in the gym erupted in cheers. Fino leapt to his feet and hugged Betinho. Even Pastor Lobato was there, bouncing up and down, cheering.

Pai and Nadine stood through the entire match, watching their son with awe, score goal after goal.

"When he touches the ball, it is like an exquisite dance!" one of the television commentators shouted into his mike.

Betinho, nearby, heard every word about his young genius.

Earlier, when Juninho trotted out on the court, the cameras were all focused on the other players, but when he left the court after the match, they were all on him. The team did not win the championship; they were runner-up. But Neymar Jr. made his mark that day on the court at Briosa.

Fino stood up from his bench on the sidelines excited. "They love him," Betinho shouted to him over the noise of the packed house.

"He spins, he twists, he stops and starts," Fino muttered. "The ball never leaves his feet. He is amazing!"

"He dances exquisitely, no?" Betinho asked.

"There is nothing I can teach him," Fino said.

"Then my advice to you is to stay out of his way," Betinho said.

Fino looked at his friend. "You're probably right. He is a genius. You, I'm not so sure about."

Betinho laughed and his whole body shook.

Then he froze when he saw Jose Ely de Miranda, the chief manager of Santos FC, known to everyone who was anyone as Zito. He was sitting in the stands, intently watching the team play. And taking notes.

"Zito!" Betinho said. "What a pleasant surprise!"

Zito noted his friend's discomfort. "Don't worry," he said, chuckling, shaking his old friend's hand. "I'm not going to take him yet. I just want to look at him."

"Who?" Betinho asked, playing dumb.

"Who else do you have out there that plays like he could be the next big thing?" Zito asked.

Betinho watched his student with unconditional love. He was proud of the boy. He hadn't felt this way since Robinho played his way into stardom. He believed in what his heart told him that first day when he was looking for his son on the beach and found Juninho instead. Here was the boy he discovered, Juninho, who the loving Brazilian fans called *Neymar* and who would soon be well-known around the world too.

A Great Education

NEYMAR STARED UP at the big building that housed the *Liceu São Paulo* on Avenida Ana Costa, painted in school colors, all red and white, and five-stories high. Pai stood with him and they were both excited. Fino was not only a coach at Briosa, he was also the head of futsal at this very expensive and exclusive private school. He offered them an appointment with the school's principal.

Tio Gil, the principal, was waiting for them when the elevator doors whispered open. "Neymar, I am so happy to finally meet you face to face!" he said, shoving out his hand. "Nice haircut."

Neymar Junior took Tio Gil's hand and shook it. He smiled at Pai. "We think you are doing a great job with your son, Mr. Silva Santos," he said to Pai and ushered them into his office. "I've seen him play many times." He closed the door behind them.

Tio Gil looked at Neymar. "I know you are playing wonderfully at Briosa, but you are still a student and you need an education. A great education. Which we can provide for you here." He was looking at Pai now. "So I have an offer for your son. A free education for both your children in exchange for Neymar playing on our futsal team."

"But my sister doesn't play soccer," Neymar said, puzzled.

"Then I have good news and more good news," said the Principal. "The good news is, you play. The other good news is, your sister doesn't. And everything here is free. We want to give you both a scholarship."

"But I would be playing on your futsal team, not grass," Neymar said.

Tio Gil smiled. "Of course." he laughed. "I understand you worked hard to get to the big field at Briosa and no one would ever take that away from you. I am just hoping that you will also play on our little futsal team. It is very important to us.

There is a championship coming up and some other matches. Our team can't seem to break out and we believe you can make a difference."

Neymar looked at his dad and then back to Tio Gil. "I love futsal, sir," Neymar said. "But I don't know anybody here."

Pai could not believe his son was saying these things.

Tio Gil got a serious look on his face. "I believe you know at least one of our students," he said. "At least that's what Betinho and Fino say. His name is Dudu?"

"Dudu is here?!"

Tio Gil laughed and nodded.

Neymar took a deep breath. "When do I start?"

"Now," Tio Gil said and stood up. "Welcome to *Liceu São Paulo!*"

Tio Gil came around the desk, shook hands with Neymar Junior and Senior, then opened the door for them. Betinho and Fino, who had been listening at the door, almost fell into the room.

From that day forward, Neymar's life changed.

What had been a dull public education in Praia Grande, became a grand first class education in São Paulo. The school spared no expense to bring in the best teachers from around Brazil. Neymar could not have gotten this kind of education anywhere else. But he still had a difficult time with math. And that's where Dudu came in.

"Here, look at this," Dudu said opening his math book and showing Neymar a math problem as they hurried to class along the third-floor hallway of Liceu São Paulo. Everything at Liceu was in red and white, including the walls and the number 10 jersey Neymar wore.

"Positive integers that are greater than one and are divisible by one and themselves," Dudu said. "What are they?"

Neymar thought about it for a moment, and then said, "Prime numbers."

"Correct!" Dudu said and they high-fived.

"My father may be the best soccer tutor in the world," Neymar said as they got to the classroom door. "But you are the best math tutor."

"Finally!" Dudu said. "Something I'm better at than you." He wore the number 11 jersey. They went into the room.

Neymar took his seat. Math was the bane of his existence, even though he could calculate in his head where every other player was on the field at any given time. That was math theory and he was good at it. But math application is what he needed to master to pass the class. And that's where Dudu shined.

It was test day and Mrs. Rinaldi, his math teacher, was already up at the front of the class, hastily scribbling problems on the blackboard with a broken stick of pink chalk.

A blank sheet of paper was waiting for Neymar on his desktop. He watched Mrs. Rinaldi write on the blackboard some more and realized he understood what she was writing. Thanks to Dudu.

After the test, Dudu waited for Neymar in the hall. "Nail it?" he asked.

"Let's just say, I wasn't totally confused."

"Good enough!" Dudu said. "Let's get to practice!"

Later that day, at Briosa, in the middle of practice, Betinho waved Neymar over from the field. He was with two men in suits—the same men who had watched Neymar a few weeks back at the Portuguesa Santista futsal court.

"Juninho, I want you to meet Mr. Rodrigues and Mr. Vieira.

Neymar stuck out his hand.

"It is a pleasure to meet you, Neymar," Rodrigues said, shaking the boy's hand. "Or do you prefer to be called *Juninho?*"

Neymar studied the two men carefully. "Neymar Junior," he said.

"Great," the man said. "We were here watching you play when the fans chanted your name. Mostly the girls. We were impressed by how much they loved you."

"But more impressed by how well you played," Vieira interjected.

"So, you are here to see me?" Neymar asked.

"To see you. To speak to you. And to ask if you might be interested in playing at Meninos da Vila."

Neymar gasped. Meninos da Vila was the Santos FC Youth Academy.

"I believe you have left Mr. Neymar Junior speechless," Betinho joked.

"Are y-you talking about Santos?" Neymar asked.

Rodrigues nodded. "Interested?"

"Are you kidding? This is a dream come true!" he said, hopping around excitedly.

Vieira glanced over at Betinho, then returned his attention to Neymar. "Our friend Zito, the manager of Santos, saw you play. He could not stop talking about you."

Neymar was so excited, tears welled up in his eyes and he could not hold them back. Out on the field one of the referees blew the whistle. He spun and charged out on the field where his friend Dudu was waiting for him.

Betinho and the men from Santos watched Neymar as he danced around Dudu. He flailed his arms, shouting something they could not hear. But whatever it was, it caused Dudu to fall to the grass and writhe around like a caught fish.

Both boys laughed.

So did Betinho and Rodrigues and Vieira. "Thank you for inviting us," Rodrigues said to Betinho. "We are looking forward to many years with him."

While they were standing around, Pai arrived from work and joined the men on the sideline. He knew who they were and why they were there because he had already negotiated the terms of the deal. "Look at him out there," Pai said, pointing out his son, who was still hopping around like a wild hare. "He can hardly control himself. What did you do to my son?"

"It's not what we did to him," Betinho said. "It is what we are *going* to do. We are going to make him a star."

"We will give him a five-year contract with the Fish and a little over two hundred dollars a month," Vieira said matter-of-factly, rummaging through his leather valise, pulling out a contract. "Everything you asked for, Mr. Silva Santos."

"It means you don't have to work so hard, Pai," Betinho said. "Nadine can stay home."

Pai remained stoic. This was not the time to get emotional. He nodded.

"Betinho stays as well," he said.

"Of course," Rodrigues said.

"And so do I," insisted Pai.

"Without question. Where would he be without you two?" said Rodrigues.

Pai looked at Betinho. Everything was going according to plan. But a lot faster than they expected.

After School Practice

THE FOG IN JARDIM GLÓRIA reached up the side of the mountain from the sea and spilled over the top. The thrumming of Pai's two-stroke motorcycle engine cut through the thick silence of the early morning as he weaved a path through the streets of Praia Grande over the river into São Vicente and up Avenida Ana Costa to his son's school, Liceu São Paulo. Neymar wrapped his arms around his father's waist, held on tight, and leaned into every turn as they moved through the morning traffic.

"Faster!" Neymar shouted.

Pai laughed at his thrill-seeker son and when he pulled up in front of the Liceu, he carefully stopped the motorbike and Neymar climbed off.

"See you after school," Pai said.

"Let's go a different way to Santos this time,"

Neymar said. "The long way."

"Okay, that's a deal," Pai said. He drove his son to school then to practice every day since Neymar had signed the deal with the Santos youth club. "You want to spend more time on the bike, huh?"

Neymar shook his head. "No, I want to spend more time with you," he said, slinging his backpack over his shoulder. "See you after school." He trotted to the gate and joined up with Dudu and they both vanished in the throng of students.

After school, Neymar watched his school team get ready for practice while he waited for his dad to pick him up. The Liceu physical education teacher, Fuschini, hurried across the court, dodging players. He climbed into the stands and sat down next to him.

"You know, the whole team looks up to you," he said.

"Thanks, Mr. Fuschini," Neymar said.

"They love playing alongside you at the games," Fuschini continued.

"Me too," Neymar said, checking the clock. "I guess I better go. My dad's probably waiting for me outside." He stood up.

"Games are one thing," Fuschini went on. "Practice—that's where you get to know each other, don't you think?"

"Yeah, I guess so," Neymar said absently, anxious to leave.

"I was talking to a few of the guys the other day. They miss training with you."

"They said that?" Neymar was surprised.

"They think you don't like training with them. Like maybe you're too good for them."

"That's not true, sir," Neymar said.

"Like I said—they look up to you," Fuschini said.

"But, I can't train! I have to be at Vila Belmiro!" Neymar exclaimed.

"I'm just telling you what some of them wished for, that's all. I know you have to go," said Fuschini.

The whole conversation left Neymar feeling terrible.

Pai appeared at the top of the stairs and looked around, finally spotting his son in the stands near the court. "Juninho! What are you doing?

We're late!" he called.

Neymar looked up at his father, then out on the court and met Dudu's eyes. He looked over at Fuschini, then made a decision, stood up and put down his backpack. "Can I ditch today, Dad?"

"Ditch?" Pai said, coming down the rows of seats toward his son. "What do you mean, *ditch?*"

"I want to train with the guys," Neymar said. "It's been a long time."

Pai stopped and looked out on the court. The team had stopped their warm-ups and stood still, hanging on their every word. He realized in that instant that they wanted him to stay. And Neymar realized he wanted to be with them.

Fuschini pretended to write something in his journal. He liked letting the boys sort these things out themselves, once he'd said his piece. But he listened intently.

"Well, you know what, son? I think that's a *great* idea," Pai finally said.

All the boys on the floor erupted with a cheer that echoed around the gym.

Neymar charged down the steps two at a time and jumped out onto the court. His teammates immediately surrounded him.

"Okay, who knows what a *dar um chapéu* is?" he asked.

A bunch of hands went up.

A friendly game commenced. Dudu captained one side, Neymar headed up the other. Two guys marked Neymar the minute he made his move, but he got the ball anyway and charged the goal. The defenders tried helplessly to block his way and he lobbed the ball over their heads and plowed through them as the ball landed behind them. *"That* is a *dar um chapéu!"* he shouted.

Dudu laughed. No one could touch his friend when it came to skills. He was proving it right out on the pitch.

The goalkeeper charged but the ball went between his legs in a perfect nutmeg and into the goal before he could do anything.

"Dar um caneta!" he shouted. "Nutmeg!"

Half the guys stopped playing and just watched

their superstar teammate go through his moves.

"Get into the game!" Fuschini shouted from the sideline.

"We can't help it, Coach!" one player said as Dudu raced by behind him and shot the ball to Neymar.

"He's amazing!" said another.

After the practice, the boys all came up to Neymar as one group and surrounded him. "Thanks for practicing with us," Dudu said and the rest of the boys nodded.

"It was like playing for the Seleção today. We must have been crazy thinking you needed to train with us."

Neymar grinned and shook all their hands. "I had fun. And I just want you to know that I don't see myself as anything other than a part of our team. Remember that." It was something his father always taught him, ever since he was a little kid, playing in the street. "We're all equals out there and we all want the same thing, right?"

"To win!" Dudu shouted.

And everyone cheered.

Fuschini stayed on the sideline and watched his team, then leaned against the railing and smiled to himself, pleased.

Pai waited at the door and when Juninho passed, they high-fived and both of them left the court for the day.

Madrid

NOT LONG AFTER Neymar joined the newly created
U13 squad at Santos FC in 2004, Antonio Lima dos
Santos, also known as Lima, was already talking
about creating a U15 squad. Lima had been a striker
who played more than 700 games for Santos. As
a new Santos coach, he conferred with Zito. They
needed to keep their star, Neymar, challenged.
Everyone in the Santos organization knew that
Neymar always flourished playing on squads above
his age group. He was also getting offers from
teams all around the world. Santos needed to keep
Neymar and let him grow into the first team.

Neymar made friends easily and it wasn't long
before he and Paulo Henrique Ganso, known
affectionately as P.H., became best friends when
the tall attacking midfielder arrived at Santos from

Paysandu in 2005. P.H. was the perfect partner on the field for Neymar and they were brilliant together.

A few months later, Neymar got an agent, Wagner Ribeiro. A year after that, in 2006, almost to the day, Ribeiro hand-delivered a letter to Neymar from Real Madrid. It included two airline tickets to Spain for Neymar Sr. and Neymar Jr.

Real Madrid Technical Secretary Ramon Martinez had heard about the genius from Mogi das Cruzes through his Brazilian scouts and wanted to see the 14-year-old for a tryout. Martinez talked his new boss, Fernando Martin, into flying them out. Betinho was sworn to secrecy. Santos could not know. If they asked, he wasn't allowed to spill the beans.

On the big day, Betinho drove them to the airport.

"Relax," said Betinho. "Enjoy yourself. And say hello to Fernando Martin for me."

"Do you know him?" Pai asked.

"No. That's why I want you to say hello for me. Tell him 'Betinho says hi' and tell him what I do and how much I mean to you!"

Pai burst out laughing.

The tryout on the field at Valdebebas, the Real Madrid training grounds, was a huge success and the next day Neymar and his father watched a match between Real Madrid and Deportivo La Coruna from the VIP Box. Real Madrid was winning 4–0 when the folded piece of paper made its way to their box via messenger. Pai read it and collapsed back in his seat in shock. He looked at his son and shakily showed him the note.

"What is it, Dad?" Neymar asked.

"They want to sign you," he said. "They'll have papers ready in three days. All we have to think about is your price."

Neymar felt his stomach tighten. He looked around the field and took a deep breath. He was unsure. He was only fourteen. He was afraid, but he hid it from his father. He didn't want to disappoint him.

Two days later, on March 29, 2006, Neymar looked at the papers on the table.

Pai signed and handed the pen to his son, who signed his name. The next day, on March 30th, Neymar belonged to Real Madrid on paper. The financials were the only thing left to negotiate.

Neymar trained with Dani Carvajal, a right back; Pablo Sarabia, a midfielder; and Alex Fernandez, another midfielder. Neymar only knew Portuguese and the others, all Spaniards, only spoke Spanish, but all of them understood the language of soccer. Neymar played well and scored over 20 goals during their training sessions, but before the trial-training period was halfway over, his anxiety grew.

At the end of the week, at their hotel, before he went to sleep, Pai came over to his son's bedside, just as he did every night since he was a little boy. They liked to talk through the day. Neymar learned from Pastor Lobato to go over the day and if he hurt anyone, to make sure he prayed for them and prayed to find a way to make amends to that person. This time, however, Pai did all the talking.

"They love you here," he said.

"They don't love *me*. They love the way I play," Neymar said.

"Exactly," Pai said with a smile. "But I need you to listen. Real Madrid wants you to stay. They have offered to set you up in an exclusive private school here. Rafaella too.

"We already go to a private school," Neymar said and looked into his father's eyes. That was where he always found solace and answers.

"I know that look," Pai said. "I'm on to you."

"Well, you always want me to be truthful, right?"

"The whole truth and nothing but the truth," Pai replied.

"I miss Mom and Rafaella. And my teammates. I miss Santos."

Pai studied his son for a long time, then finally nodded. "I miss them too, son," he confessed to Neymar. He missed his wife too. He could not see living here either. It was a difficult decision, but it had to be made. He knew that his 14-year-old was unhappy in Madrid. He wasn't himself. He didn't smile. And being in one of the best clubs in the world wasn't as important to him as his son's happiness. His gut told him that maybe it was too early to leave Santos and their family home and move to Spain. He knew that his son was a great player. So it would be best to let him grow where he felt more at home. Where he was happy. And when he was more mature, he could decide when and where he was ready to play in Europe.

Juninho fell asleep and Pai watched him sleep. He loved his son so much and he immediately knew what he had to do.

Pai called Ribeiro, Neymar's agent back home. "He's too young, Wagner. He needs to grow up and the best place for him is back home, playing for Santos."

"Just as well. Real won't pay any good money for Juninho anyway," Ribeiro said.

Pai chuckled. "Then bring us home. But how do we get out of the agreement?"

"Tell you what," Ribeiro said on the other end of the phone. "I'll ask for 60,000 Euros."

"They will never agree to that!" Pai said.

"Exactly," the agent said.

The next day, after a short conversation with the people in charge at Real Madrid, Ribeiro hung up the phone and immediately called his client to give him the good news. Real Madrid decided they did not want Neymar da Silva Santos, Junior after all.

Juninho was excited and wanted to pack right away.

"One more thing, Wagner," Pai said.

"What do you want? First class tickets? I already got them."

"No," Pai said calmly. "It's time to reel in Santos."

There was a long pause at the other end of the phone. The silence stretched all the way from Madrid to Brazil. "I think I know what you mean. Want me to call the President of Santos?"

"No, that won't be necessary," Pai said. "I'll speak with him myself."

There was another long, loud silence.

"All right, Pai," Ribeiro said at the other end of the line. "I hope you know what you are doing."

"Don't worry, I do," Pai said and hung up.

Five minutes later, Marcelo Teixeira, the President of Santos took the call from Neymar's father and two minutes after that, he did not know what hit him.

"We are in Madrid, Marcelo," Pai said. "And Real Madrid wants our boy."

There was a different kind of silence this time—

the kind that accompanies a realization. "We have been very good to your family, Pai," Teixeira said. It wasn't a threat. It couldn't be. Pai held all the cards.

"We think of you as family too, Marcelo," Pai finally said into the phone. "We will stay, if you make things right."

Teixeira cleared his throat. He knew exactly what Pai was saying. "Neymar is like a son to me. To all of us," Teixeira finally said. "Who am I to deny a son anything?" He already knew Chelsea was also trying to get into the mix and he needed to head this off at the pass.

The next day, Carlos Martinez de Albornoz, the Director General of Real Madrid sat pensively in his office and wondered if he had just made the biggest mistake of his life.

When Neymar and his father returned home, two things happened: Santos created a U15 squad to retain their shining star. And overnight, Neymar became a millionaire when Santos FC signed a new contract for 1.2 million Euros for five years with a buyout clause of around 45 million Euros.

Neymar Jr. and Ronaldo
The Phenomenon

On March 9, 2009, Neymar sat on the bench, not knowing if he was playing or not. His new manager, Vagner Mancini, would not say. Earlier that week, Santos FC moved him up to the first team.

Pai had some advice for him when he heard the news: "Watch your back. These big guys are going to want to turn you into Neymar *feijoada,*" he quipped. *Feijoada* was the national dish of Brazil, a stew of beans with beef and pork. Neymar knew his dad was kidding, but he definitely did not want to end up sitting in a giant bowl with chunks of spicy Juninho instead of pork.

He scanned the stands and although he could not see them, he knew his parents and sister were in the box seats at Pacaembu, the municipal stadium in São Paulo. Santos was playing Oeste, the team from Itápolis, a small municipality in the center of São Paulo.

He heard the fans shouting his name, but Mancini seemed to be ignoring them. Then, with the score tied at 1–1, thirteen minutes into the second half, Mancini turned to Neymar and pointed at him.

Neymar joyously leapt to his feet, slapped some hands, and loped to Mancini. "Believe in yourself kid," his coach said. "Give us a goal."

Neymar nodded and when he took to the pitch, the stands at Pacaembu rumbled and shook like a major earthquake and the fans screamed his name over and over.

"NEEEEYYYYYYMMMMMAAAAARRRRRRR!!! NEEYYYYMMMMAARRRRRR!!!"

Wearing the black and white striped jersey of Santos FC with the number 18 on the back, his moment had arrived. Within seconds, he got the ball, charged toward the opposing goal, and fired a shot that hit the crossbar and bounced out.

The score was still 1–1.

But his arrival on the pitch gave Santos a shot in
the arm and they managed to score again to win
the match 2–1. Neymar had done his job and when
he left the pitch after the match, the crowd was
on its feet cheering him wildly. Their new star had
debuted and they were there to witness it.

Eight days later, on March 15, 2009, Neymar
got his chance again, this time against Mogi-Mirim,
and once more at Pacaembu. This time he wore the
number 7. Seventeen minutes after he took the field
he got the ball and took his shot, but Marcelo Cruz,
the Mogi goalkeeper, blocked it.

By the end of the first half, the match was tied at
0–0. Then P.H. Ganso got the ball in the eleventh
minute and scored and twelve minutes later
Ronaldo took it all the way and Santos was up 2–0.

A few minutes later, Molina came across the
halfway line and passed the ball to Germano, who
went left and shot it to Triguinho who then blazed
into the center. Neymar came out from between
the pack of defenders who had been marking him

and dove at the ball, heading it into the back of the net! 3–0!

He had scored his first goal for Santos! He ran around with pure joy on his face, his index finger pointing to the heavens in honor of his grandfather. He had made a promise to his father to dedicate his first goal to his grandfather and he kept his promise. Then he jumped into the air and punched the sky, imitating Pelé, who had played in Santos for many years.

Neymar charged over to P.H., leapt into his arms, and hugged him.

"The kid from Santos shines!" Milton Leite, the announcer from Sports TV, shouted into his microphone. "This is a historic goal, right here! This is a historic date for Brazilian football!"

As Neymar left the field, Glenda Kozlowski, a former athlete and now a TV personality, stuck a microphone in his face. "You've got your first goal for the first team, Neymar. What's next?"

"What's next? Stop by next Sunday," Neymar said into the mic. "We're playing Corinthians. We are playing Ronaldo!"

"Ronaldo is over the hill and chubby," the announcer said. "Do you seriously think he has a chance against you?"

Neymar didn't like what she had to say about his hero, so he smiled. "I hope so," he said and hurried into the dressing room. What was she saying? Ronaldo had not only brought Brazil their last World Cup trophy in 2002, he had won the World Cup in 1994 and was the FIFA Player of the Year three times!

"There you have it," Glenda said. "Neymar. Some are already calling him the next Pelé!"

The following Sunday at Vila Belmiro, Neymar took the field against the Corinthians and faced off against his hero, Ronaldo. Just before he went out, he and his father recited the verse from Isaiah.

It was the Phenomenon's last game and he fought hard to win it. Santos lost. Ronaldo got within twenty yards of the goal and, with the heart of a true champion, brilliantly shot the ball into the net.

Neymar stood on the field and watched the goal in awe. "Amazing," he said to P.H.

"What'd you expect? It's his last game. You think the Phenomenon is going to go out with a whimper?"

"Thank God he didn't!" Neymar said.

"Shhh," P.H. said. "Here he comes."

Ronaldo came off the field for the last time in his career and when he passed Neymar and P.H, he winked. "It's been fun!" he said.

From Hero to Zero

THE FOLLOWING JANUARY, when Neymar and André Felipe Ribeiro de Souza walked onto the field for the opener of the 2010 season, the entire audience laughed and their raucous catcalls shook the stands.

They both had brand new matching Mohawk haircuts. They stopped on the sideline to let the audience take them in. "I don't like it," André said, running his hand through the mop of hair on the top of his head.

"Nobody likes a whiner," Neymar kidded. "But it looks like *everybody* likes a Mohawk."

André laughed.

P.H. Ganso and Robinho, the fourth member of the Santos *fearsome foursome,* jogged over and P.H. was not happy when he saw their haircuts. "I hope you don't think *I'm* going to get one of those," he said as the four of them trotted onto the field.

"Yeah, hey, I was just getting used to that smudge thing you had," Robinho said, wiping the front of his head, then ruffling Neymar's hair. "But that is just plain ridiculous."

"We're trying to get noticed," Neymar half-joked as they took their positions.

"Noticed?" Robinho said. "Listen, man. It won't be long and you'll be coming to work in a helicopter."

Robinho did not know how right he was. In the next three months, Neymar scored 14 goals during the Campeonato Paulista, known as the Paulistão, the professional soccer league championship in São Paulo, and by April, he had his own chopper to get him from one place to the next. He became everyone's hero in those three months.

And then it all fell apart.

During a game with Atletico Goianiense in May, he wasn't picked to take a penalty kick he thought he deserved and threw a tantrum. He went after the team captain and the coach, and his drama on the pitch hit all the newspapers. They dubbed him the *Neymonster.* When he left the field that day his mother was waiting for him outside the locker room. "This is not the son I raised," she said.

Neymar Jr. was ashamed. He had totally lost it. "I'm sorry, Mom. I know I was wrong," he said.

"Yes, you were wrong and now you're going to make it right," she spat back. "Get back in there and make amends."

Neymar returned to the locker room and apologized to both teams and when he did, the coach, Dorival Junior, took him aside for a chat. "Look, three months ago no one knew your name and now everyone wants a piece of you. I know what that's like and I understand what you're going through. But you need to focus on the game. Game. Not fame. I can't guarantee it will ever get any easier for you. The only thing that's easy is to go from hero to zero. Your job is to play, not throw tantrums. I'm suspending you for two games." He turned and walked away.

"Yes sir," Neymar said. He knew he deserved it.

Goal of the Year

NEYMAR *AND* P.H. were not selected for the 2010 South Africa World Cup national squad. Five-time winner Brazil got eliminated in the quarterfinals and Coach Dunga was replaced with Mano Menezes, a tough-looking man with short-cropped hair. Two days after he took over the Seleção, Menezes called Neymar to the squad he was building for the upcoming World Cup in Brazil in 2014.

The following month they all went to the Meadowlands in New Jersey to play the USA in a friendly match. Menezes included P.H. Ganso and Robinho for the New Jersey game. At least three of the foursome from Santos' most successful years ever were reunited for their first outing with the Seleção. It was August 10, 2010.

Not known for mincing words, Menezes' advice

was short and sweet. "Play the game you know, boys. Play the game you know."

In the 28th minute, Robinho passed to André Santos as he charged left and when he saw that Neymar had beat his defender to the box, André crossed the ball to Neymar who headed it into the net. He immediately looked surprised as if he didn't expect to score.

Neymar dropped to his knees, raised his arms into the sky, and kissed the Brazilian crest on his jersey. A moment later, his teammates piled all over him. He knew right then and there that it was the first step on his journey to the 2014 World Cup and he was the happiest man alive. Less than a year later, on July 27, 2011, Neymar stepped out on the pitch at Vila Belmiro where Santos faced Flamengo in the twelfth round of the Brasileirão, the country's premier soccer competition. The famous Clube de Regatas do Flamengo from Rio de Janeiro and Santos were bitter rivals and Flamengo had already won the title six times.

Ronaldinho played for Flamengo and scored a hat

trick. But for a brief moment, Neymar had center stage. There was only a half hour left in the match.

Neymar saw Leo Moura and Williams out of the corner of his eye as he stole the ball. They marked him like a pair of vultures. He had to break free. Then the opportunity came. He made a run and passed Renato who tried to block him, but Neymar was too fast and squeezed by only to come face to face with Ronaldo Angelim, the Flamengo center back. In a split-second, he dribbled, flicked the ball to one side and took the other. Then just as the defenders dove at him and the goalkeeper came off his line, he fired it into the back of the net. The roar of the crowd seemed to go on forever.

The following January of 2012, Neymar was nominated for the Puskas Award for that Flamengo goal. He went to Zurich for the FIFA Ballon D'Or awards, which is an annual award given to a male player who is considered to have played the best soccer in the previous year. He was up against Leo Messi and Wayne Rooney for the Puskas Award for goal of the year. As far as Neymar was concerned, he did not have a chance. Nevertheless, deep down inside him there was a burning ember of hope.

So, when they announced his name as the winner and flashed his face on the big screen monitor, he almost threw up.

Hugo Sanchez, from Mexico, handed him the trophy. Neymar could not believe it. He admired the shiny trophy and saw his reflection and the comma scar above his eyebrow: the accident scar. He steeled his nerves, and then spoke into the microphone. "I am very happy that you have given me this award. I was up against two of the greatest players in the world. I am a huge fan of both of them!" He tried to hold back the tears. "I want to thank God and all those who are here tonight. I hope you enjoy your evening."

The applause was loud. He looked to where he would leave the stage, and there was Pelé, the greatest player in the history of soccer, backstage, waiting for him. When Neymar stepped up to him, Pelé took him by the shoulders and congratulated him, then whispered in his ear, "Now it is time to go and play in Europe."

When he got back from Switzerland, his family was excited because a TV commercial he had made before he left was going to air. They couldn't wait to see it. The family sat on the edges of their seats waiting for the commercial to play.

"Okay, this is it," Pai said, "Everybody be quiet."

It was a commercial for a product his parents knew very well: Neymar was the new spokesperson for Panasonic Water Purifiers.

Everyone laughed when the commercial was over. Everyone but Neymar. He wasn't sure why they were laughing. "Hey, maybe I'm not such a great actor but I thought I did pretty good!" he pleaded.

"We're not laughing at you, Juninho," Nadine said. "We are laughing because a long time ago, when the lights were out because we couldn't pay the bill, your father sold those purifiers door-to-door."

"What?!" Neymar said.

"For minimum wage!" Pai announced proudly. "And now, they are paying you millions to sell them!"

Everyone laughed again.

Winds of Change

In September, 2012, P.H. came to Neymar with some news.

"I'm leaving Santos, Juninho," P.H. said. "I wanted you to be the first to know."

"Why?" Neymar asked, horrified. "Did they cut you?"

P.H. laughed. "No, man. I just signed a deal with São Paulo."

Neymar hugged his best friend. He felt both devastated and ecstatic at the same time. "I don't know what I am going to do without you. Nobody knows me on the pitch like you," he said, fighting back the tears.

"Wait until I square off against you," P.H. joked. "You'll wish I didn't."

Neymar and P.H. shared a laugh and a hug.

"Brother against brother," Neymar said and pretended to be okay. But deep down inside, he knew that, just as it was the end of an era for P.H. on the Santos team, it was an ending for him as well. "What are you going to do?" Neymar asked his friend.

P.H. shrugged. "Who knows? Maybe I'll get married. What about you?"

"I'm working on the institute. In Praia Grande. For the kids."

"For the kids?! But you're such a selfish brat!" P.H. chided him.

"Hey, I was, I won't deny it," Neymar said. "But I've thought about this ever since I was a little kid playing in the street. When the lights got turned off because we couldn't pay the bill. We had so little back then and now I have so much. But there are still so many kids out there in Jardim Glória and all over Praia Grande. They have nothing. Less than nothing. This trip I've been on, getting the award, I've had plenty of time to think. I've realized a bunch of things."

"Oh yeah? A bunch of things?" P.H. asked. "Name one."

"Well, for one, I realized that when I was at my worst..."

"...Being a selfish brat," P.H. interjected.

"Exactly. I was just thinking of me. But I found out when I stopped thinking of me and started thinking of others, I got better. So I'm going to do what I promised I would do when I was a kid in that dark house with all those candles. I bought land in Praia Grande. Lots of it. For poor kids to come and play soccer and learn the game. It's going to be a sports school and I've found some teachers to help. I want you to help too. We are going to have soccer and volleyball and swimming and judo and basketball and reading and writing and computer science. And music. Beautiful music. There are so many grown-ups who can't read or write. I want to change that."

P.H. studied his friend for a long silent moment, then hugged him. "I'm in, brother," he said. "But watch out. I'm also coming to get you!"

And true to his word, six months later, In February 2013, Santos faced off in a friendly against São Paulo. Neymar was excited to play against his best friend in the whole world, P.H., who had been doing fairly well defending for São Paulo for the past six months. It was time for a little brother against brother action. But when P.H. took the field, the Santos fans jeered him and hundreds screamed cat-calls at him. They shouted that he was a sell-out and threw coins at him.

When a couple of fans jumped the fence, charged after P.H., and looked like they were going to attack him, Neymar rushed in and stood his ground with his best friend. "Stay calm!" he shouted repeatedly and finally the fans calmed down and the game could begin. "Ousadia e alegria!" he cried out. It was his and P.H.'s motto in life. Ousadia meant daring as in daring to do something new, and *alegria* meant to be happy: happy to be playing football and happy to be alive. The fans calmed down and the game resumed, much to P.H.'s relief.

A few months later, on May 27, it was Neymar's

turn to play one last game with Santos and bid farewell to his home team of nine years. But before he did, the day before, he took a helicopter to Tabatinga Beach and stood up as best man at P.H.'s wedding.

The next day, Neymar faced a difficult choice. With two offers on the table from Real Madrid and Barcelona, Neymar had to decide. He was ready. No matter which team he chose, he was going to Europe. He heard Pelé's voice in his head again from the night he won the Puskas award: *Go to Europe.* The following day he went to Brasilia with Santos for his final game with the Fish. The new Mané Garrincha Stadium would be the venue for Neymar's last match with Santos. It was also to be the home stadium of the 2014 World Cup. It was a sellout. Over 63,000 fans showed up. Neymar came with 229 matches behind him, 138 goals, and six titles. The curtain was coming down on nine years with Santos FC.

Tears rolled down his face. Victor Andrade and Rafael, two of his teammates, stood on either side of him for support. The rest of the team surrounded him. "I want to thank all of you for the moments we've had together; the training sessions, the victories, and the titles. It is not easy for me to leave you, but I am living my dream. I wanted to play today—to have one last chance to play 90 minutes with you—whether we win or lose. Thank you all for everything. I will always be your fan," he said, tears streamed down his face and he pointed to each team member. "I wish you all the best. I will always be your friend and I will always support you, wherever I am."

That night, after the match, a match that ended in a draw, 0–0, he announced to the world that he was going to Barcelona FC.

But before he left for Barça, he would play for Brazil and establish his place on the National team. He was looking forward to the Confederations Cup on June 30, 2013.

Here Comes Number 10

THE CONFEDERATIONS CUP was Neymar's chance to take on the most cherished role in Brazilian soccer by playing on the big stage at home against the champions of each continent. The Confederations Cup was a dress rehearsal for Brazil exactly one year before the World Cup. Neymar was excited to prove to his fellow countrymen and to the world that he could lead them to the World Cup trophy. Coach Luiz Felipe "Big Phil" Scolari, who won, with Brazil, the World Cup in 2002, replaced Mano Menezes as the Seleção coach by the end of 2012 and everyone cheered.

Scolari's first move was to give Neymar the number 10 jersey. Neymar understood its significance. Number 10 was Pelé's number. When Scolari handed Neymar the jersey, he gave him the opportunity and the responsibility. He entrusted him to lead the team to win the World Cup. Neymar was only 20. But he felt he was ready.

From the very start, the Confederations Cup was a huge success for Brazil and Neymar. They beat Japan 3–0 in the opening game, with goals from Neymar in the 3rd minute, Paulinho in the 48th minute, and Jô in the 90th. Three days later, the team beat Mexico with Neymar scoring again in the 9th minute.

Brazil went on to defeat Uruguay 2–1 in the semifinal with goals from Fred in the 41st minute, paired with a late goal from Paulinho in the 86th minute.

Then came the final against the World Champions —Spain.

It was a strange feeling for Neymar when he walked through the tunnel of the famed Estádio do Maracanã in Rio De Janeiro. He was about to play his future teammates from Barcelona. Players he admired—Xavi, Iniesta, Busquets, Pedro, and Pique—were all there. He exchanged looks and hugs. Just a few weeks after this game, he would share the same locker room at Camp Nou with them and they would become his friends and teammates. But today he was a man on a mission. It was nice, he thought. If they could beat the world champions at home, it would show his future teammates how good he was.

It was almost 7pm. Game time.

Out on the field, everyone said Big Phil Scolari looked relaxed when he shook Spanish manager Vicente del Bosque's hand.

Neymar closed his eyes and visualized the coming match. He made himself alone for a few moments, even though he was surrounded by his teammates, Fred, Alves, Cesar, Silva, Luiz, Marcelo, Oscar, Luiz Gustavo, Paulinho, and Hulk. Dani draped his arm over his friend's shoulder to steady him.

The Brazilian national anthem played and the team and the fans started singing. But according to FIFA rules, national anthems are limited to 90 seconds. At this match, when the 90 seconds were up, the song was only two-thirds through. The music cut out, but the fans and team kept singing, *a cappella,* until the anthem was finished.

Dani Alves quietly mouthed a prayer to Neymar and Neymar was grateful and relaxed. The team took to their positions and Neymar went to the centerline.

Two minutes later, Neymar assisted and Fred got the ball, fell, and while he was on the ground, kicked the ball past Casillas and Brazil took the lead, 1–0.

Forty-one minutes later, Oscar passed the ball to Neymar on the left side of the penalty area. Neymar shot left-footed and bent it over Casillas' head and into the net.

The crowd went crazy when Neymar the Wizard strengthened their lead 2–0. Two minutes into the second half, Fred repeated his first two-minute goal by curving the ball inside the far post from the left. Casillas got his fingers on it but it was too hard and too fast and it slipped from his grasp and fell into the net. Brazil won 3–0. And when Neymar walked off the field, all 63,000 fans cheered.

A few days later, Neymar stood in front of 56,500 fans in Barcelona, a record turnout for a Brazilian player. While he mentally prepared to play alongside his hero, Leo Messi, he knew it was going to be the most challenging year of his life.

The Way Home

NEYMAR'S FIRST SEASON in Barça ended with mixed results. He scored 15 goals in 41 appearances under new coach Gerardo (Tata) Martino. The fans and the media watched him closely to see how he fit into the Barça system and how he teamed up with Leo Messi.

The season ended in disappointment as Barça failed to reach the Champions League trophy and the Copa del Rey trophy. Their only hope was the La Liga championship, which came down to the last game of the season.

Although Alexis scored the first goal, Barça was ultimately unable to lift their fifth title in six years, as Atletico Madrid held them to a 1–1 draw at Camp Nou and won the league. Barça ended with a second place finish. Godin's header equalizer after

the break was enough to give the visitors the point
and the title.

Neymar was on the bench until the 61st minute
when Tata called him to replace Pedro, but he
could not break through the tight Atletico defense.

A few days later, the players had their last
meeting then geared up to return to their home
teams. Messi, Neymar, Alexis, Mascherano, and
the Spanish players all said farewell to each other
and wished each other success in the World Cup.
Neymar and Dani Alves joined the Brazilian team.
Almost everyone on the Barça main roster was
heading for Brazil in a few days to represent their
respective countries on the biggest stage of all.

"You know what I wish for?" Neymar told Messi
before they left to return to their home countries.

"Yes. That Brazil wins the World Cup,"
answered Messi.

Neymar grinned. "Sure, but I would love to have
Brazil and Argentina play each other in the finals.
You and I against each other."

Messi, the captain of the Argentinian team,

agreed with a smile. "Yes, it would be cool to beat you on your home turf!"

The two laughed and hugged each other.

In 1950, Brazil hosted the World Cup for the first time. Everyone in Brazil felt at the time that this was their team moment in history, winning the World Cup on home soil. The Seleção made it to the final against Uruguay at Estádio do Maracanã in Rio that time, needing only a draw to win the World Cup. Prior to the match, Portuguese newspaper *O Mundo* prematurely declared Brazil *the world champions.* However, in one of the biggest upsets in football history, Uruguay scored with only 11 minutes remaining, to win the match and the Cup. For Uruguay, the game went down in history as *The Maracanazo.* The match led to a period of national mourning and went down in history as a catastrophe. This upset was the motivator for a big change to the National team, but even five World Cup wins in later years could not wipe this scar from their soccer history. For Brazil, hosting another World Cup after

54 years was an opportunity to finally remove the scar. The success in the Confederations Cup a year earlier led to the belief that this team could achieve the dream and bring the trophy back. For Neymar, a win at the Maracanã was a dream he was ready to achieve. Although he was born years after the disaster of *The Maracanazo,* he knew the story like everyone in Brazil. Just prior to the first game of the World Cup he said, "We want to fulfill the dreams of all Brazilians, which is to win the World Cup."

He meant it, and he believed that the team with the greatest home support could do it.

Neymar became the symbol of hope for two hundred million Brazilians. They admired him for his speed, his playful creative talent, and respected his achievements: 31 goals and 22 assists in just 49 appearances for his country. For the Brazilians, he was the golden boy from Santos, where he scored 136 goals in 225 appearances. And when the World Cup began, the entire country was madly in love with their new number 10.

Before the first game against Croatia, Neymar told his mother he would give her the number 10 shirt he would wear at the game. And he kept his word. After the game, he gave her the shirt off his back. Nadine deserved it for all the years she and Pai wrapped their boy in love and support. In this opening game of the tournament, Neymar scored two goals and the country and the entire world burst with admiration for their shining superstar.

"I'm very happy, really happy," Neymar said after the game. "This is more than I ever dreamed of and it was crucial to begin a tournament of this stature with a win. I'm happy with the two goals, but the whole team deserves a pat on the back because we kept our cool and came from behind. It's not down to just one, two, or three players; it's the team as a whole that works."

The second game with Mexico ended scoreless and Neymar knew would be remembered by the heroics of the Mexican goalkeeper, Memo Ochoa.

In the third game, against Cameroon, Neymar

scored two goals and Brazil won 4–1 and secured its place in the round of sixteen. The entire nation felt they were living the dream. Everyone wore Neymar shirts. Hopes grew from game to game. They all trusted Neymar to bring them to the Promised Land.

"How are you?" Neymar Senior asked his son after the third game.

"I'm living a dream, Dad. I am achieving the goal we had since you taught me to touch the ball when I was still crawling on the floor," said Neymar.

Neymar Senior laughed.

"And you know what?" Neymar said, "I don't feel any pressure. I'm doing what I've always dreamed of doing, and I am enjoying myself. I want to help my teammates by scoring goals, defending, challenging them for the ball, whatever is needed to get us the win."

"That's my boy," said Pai. He always taught him to be a team player. He admired his son's ability to see the bigger picture: to see himself as part of the team and the country. It always amazed Pai how he dealt with the pressure.

The first knockout game against Chile was tough and challenging. It went into overtime and penalties following a 1–1 tie. Neymar scored his penalty with a stutter-step approach that confused the keeper, then made the hit. Big Phil said that the way he scored the penalty was as if he was playing in a neighborhood game, oblivious to the enormous pressure.

Brazil's goalkeeper Julio Cesar's two saves in the shootout sent the Seleção into the quarterfinal and emotionally sent the team and the entire nation into the stratosphere. Everyone was in tears. A penalty shootout is cruel and they had looked into the abyss of elimination and survived.

Shattered Dreams, New Hopes

NEYMAR SENIOR WATCHED James Rodriguez score his sixth goal of the World Cup tournament for Columbia from the penalty spot. Brazil led 2–1 and he hoped it was going to be enough to remain there. James was one of the new rising stars of the tournament and Neymar Senior admired his skills. Colombia was a great team, one of the best in the tournament, and there was still enough time on the clock to do some damage.

The game itself was very physical and at times violent from both teams. But the referee refused to bring out the yellow and red cards from his shirt pocket. All over the world, commentators and analysts were saying that the referee should be more forceful and control the players. Foul after foul were given, stopping the flow as the game became more and more aggressive. And then, seven minutes after the Colombian goal, in the 88th minute, Neymar Senior leapt to his feet in horror when he saw his son go down, screaming in agony, gripping his back. The big screen replay showed Columbian defender Juan Núñiga come up from behind and hit Neymar with his knee.

Neymar Junior never saw it coming. He had positioned himself in the Brazilian third, taking control of the ball and then without warning all the air rushed out of his lungs as he was pushed to the ground. There was sharp pain, the worst pain he had ever felt.

Juan Núñiga tumbled around him and moved on with the ball, only to lose it. Neymar Junior shoved his hand to the small of his back, unable to hold back the tears because it hurt so badly.

Neymar Senior stood in the stands, motionless and horrified. He had a sinking, panicked feeling in the pit of his stomach. He had had this feeling before; all those years ago when Juninho was just four months old. The accident. The pain. The fear.

Marcelo charged over to his fallen teammate, straddled him, and shouted to him. "How do you feel?"

Neymar cried out, "I can't feel my legs!"

Crying helped ease the pain and he was grateful that Marcelo was there. There was no way he could get up on his own.

They called the team doctors.

Neymar Junior knew his game was over. He hoped that he would recover for the rest of the tournament.

But the pain was agonizing. He couldn't move.

Somewhere nearby he heard Núñiga shouting that he was sorry, but he could not turn to see anything. All he could see was the grass he had fallen on.

He felt every bounce as the medical team rushed him off the field on the stretcher. He had experienced this before, but never with this much pain. They brought him to the treatment room to take care of the pain. When they shoved him into the back of the waiting ambulance and the team doctors piled in after him, he caught a glimpse of his father just before the rear door slammed shut and they sped off, his father growing small in the window as they headed for the hospital. One of the emergency medical team orderlies set up an IV, someone else gave him an injection, and finally, the pain began to subside.

In the ambulance, rushing to the hospital, it became clear: his lifelong dream of going all the way to the World Cup final with the Seleção might be over.

Brazil won the game against Colombia. There was one more game to win and then the finals. Only two games to win the biggest trophy of all.

First they had to beat Germany without their best defender, team captain Thiago Silva, who was eliminated from further competition on a second yellow card in the Columbian game, and their star, Neymar.

Many thought it would be a tall order to beat Germany, which was showing itself to the world as one of the best teams in the tournament.

Completing the mission without Neymar and Silva made it look almost impossible. But the team and the nation believed they could overcome these setbacks.

The hope of the nation for Neymar's well-being, prayers for his recovery, and optimism about the upcoming game with Germany were coming from all of Brazil's two hundred million citizens.

Soon crushing news would engulf the country.

Neymar watched the crucial match from his home with family and friends. He grew tearful when his teammates, Julio Cesar and David Luiz, held up his jersey while singing the Brazilian national anthem. He hoped and prayed his teammates would make this win happen.

There was a warning sign in the 11th minute. Unmarked, Thomas Müller scored the first goal due to a big mistake by the Brazilian defense. They still had plenty of time to fight back, but no one could have predicted what happened next.

In just six minutes, Germany scored four more goals, starting with Klose's goal in the 23rd, followed by two more by Kroos at the 24th and 26th and finally with Kaedira's at the 29th.

Game over. Neymar knew it would be impossible to come back. He sat in his home, stunned. It was more excruciating than the pain in his back. The dream had become a nightmare. In the second half, when it was 7–0, Neymar turned off the TV. He couldn't watch anymore, and missed Oscar's goal at the 90th minute.

To all of Brazil, the loss to Germany, 7–1, was an even bigger catastrophe than the one in 1950. The loss to the Netherlands 3–0 in the third place game made things worse. Neymar watched the final game from the Seleção bench and rooted for his teammates. At a certain point, he covered his face with his jersey. It was too painful to watch.

But he refused to criticize his coach and his teammates and did not agree with the disapproval of both that was flying around the media. He was, as always, a team player and he did everything he could to remain close to his team.

He supported the Seleção and took the fall with them.

Neymar was an optimist. Ever since he was a boy, he saw the bright side of a bad situation. "At 6–0, 7–0 down they could have given up," he said. "But they kept running and kept trying. I'm proud of every one of them. I'm not ashamed to be Brazilian. I'm not ashamed to be a part of this team. I am proud of my teammates."

The kid from Mogi das Cruzes was grateful. He was only 22 and there were more World Cups to come and many years left to be filled with the joy of the game. He saw great challenges and opportunities in front of him to write his name as one of the greatest footballers of all time.

When the doctor showed him the x-ray of his back, he told him he was the luckiest man on earth.

"If it had been another two centimeters down, you would be in a wheelchair for the rest of your life," the doctor said. "But you are going to be all right. In two months, you will play again."

For Neymar, a devout believer, it was clear that God had kept a watchful eye over him. All his life he had felt blessed, ever since that fateful day in the mountains when he survived that horrible car accident. He was thankful for his talents, which not only brought him fame and success, but pure joy. Now in the midst of the worst events for Brazil in the 2014 World Cup, he felt that he was blessed once more. God had given him the opportunity to recover and rise again, and dance with the ball on the field he loved so much.

To play the beautiful game. To bring joy and happiness to fans all over the world.

To keep the dream alive.

And one day, to bring the biggest trophy of all, back home.

NEYMAR'S HONORS

Club

Santos

- Campeonato Paulista (3): 2010, 2011, 2012
- Copa do Brasil (1): 2010
- Copa Libertadores (1): 2011
- Recopa Sudamericana (1): 2012

Barcelona

- Supercopa de España (1): 2013

National team

Brazil

- South American Youth Championship (1): 2011
- Superclásico de las Américas (2): 2011, 2012
- Olympic Silver Medal (1): 2012
- FIFA Confederations Cup (1): 2013

Individual

- Best Young Player of Campeonato Paulista (1): 2009
- Best Forward of Campeonato Paulista (4): 2010, 2011, 2012, 2013
- Best Forward of Campeonato Brasileiro Série A (3): 2010, 2011, 2012
- Best player of Campeonato Paulista (4): 2010, 2011, 2012, 2013
- Best player of South American Youth Championship (1): 2011
- Best player of Copa Libertadores (1): 2011
- Best player of Campeonato Brasileiro Série A (1): 2011
- Best player of Recopa Sudamericana (1): 2012
- FIFA Confederations Cup Golden Ball (1): 2013
- Young Player of the Year (1): 2011
- Campeonato Brasileiro Série A Championship Squad (3): 2010, 2011, 2012
- Copa Libertadores Championship Squad (1): 2012

- Arthur Friedenreich Award (2): 2010, 2012
- Armando Nogueira Trophy (2): 2011, 2012
- Golden Ball (1): 2011 – Best Player in Brazilian League by magazine *Placar*
- Silver Ball (2): 2010, 2011 – Best Forward in Brazilian League by magazine *Placar*
- Silver Ball hors concours (1): 2012
- Golden Boot (2): 2010, 2011, 2012 – Most goals in all competition in Brazil
- Copa do Brasil Top scorer (1): 2010
- South American Youth Championship Top scorer (1): 2011
- FIFA Club World Cup Bronze Ball (1): 2011
- South American Footballer of the Year (2): 2011, 2012
- FIFA Puskás Award (1): 2011
- Campeonato Paulista Top scorer (1): 2012
- Copa Libertadores Top scorer (1): 2012
- FIFA Confederations Cup Bronze Shoe (1): 2013
- FIFA Confederations Cup Dream Team (1): 2013
- FIFA World Cup Bronze Boot (1): 2014

WORKS CITED

"Associação Atlética Portuguesa (Santos)." *Wikipedia.* Portuguesa Santista, n.d. Web. 11 July 2014.

Atkinson, Tre. "Neymar Facts You Might Not Know." *Bleacher Report.* 6 June 2013. Web. 11 July 2014.

"Biography." *Neymar Jr Brazil and FC Barcelona 2014 RSS.* Neymarjr.net, n.d. Web. 11 July 2014.

Borden, Sam. "A Soccer Prodigy, at Home in Brazil." *The New York Times.* 09 July 2012. Web. 11 July 2014.

Caioli, L. *Neymar: The Making of the World's Greatest New Number 10.* London: Icon, 2014. Print.

"Capoeira." *Wikipedia.* Wikimedia Foundation, 07 Oct. 2014. Web. 11 July 2014.

Carnevalli, J.P. *Neymar: The Mohawk Striker and Other Stories.* Vol. 1. S3 Soccer and Samba, 2013. Print.

Carnevalli. "Neymar Childhood: Childhood Scenes
　　Neymar." *YouTube,* 24 Sept. 2013. Web.
　　11 July 2014.

Costa, Nilton. "A Trajetória de Neymar até o
　　Santos - Esporte Espetacular - 06-11-2011."
　　YouTube. 6 Nov. 2011. Web. 11 July 2014.

"Descobridor de Neymar e Robinho rejeita demissão
　　e critica presidente do Santos, Brazilian Press,
　　12 Nov. 2013.

"A Documentary on Neymar Jr." *Bellarte Futsal,*
　　n.d. Web. 11 July 2014.

Drehs, Wayne. "The Lasting Legacy of Brazil 2014."
　　World Cup Central Blog. ESPN FC, n.d. Web.
　　11 July 2014.

"Enquanto Neymar Disputa O Ouro, Ex-parças
　　Lutam Na 4ª Divisão Paulista." *Globoesporte.com.*
　　Santos and Region, 8 Oct. 2012. Web.
　　11 July 2014.

ESPN. "Neymar." *ESPN FC,* n.d. Web.
　　11 July 2014.

Fearon, Matthew. "Pele Warned Barca's 50M
　　Samba Star Neymar to Ignore Chelsea and
　　City and Go Play with Messi." *Mailonline.com.*
　　5 June 2013. Web. 11 July 2014.

"FOX Soccer Blog." *Real Madrid Rejected to Buy Neymar in 2006?* N.p., 6 Sept. 2013. Web. 11 July 2014.

"Globo TV International - Neymar - The Heir to the Crown." *Globo TV Sports,* n.d. Web. 11 July 2014.

"GREMETAL; Grêmio Recreativo dos Metalúrgicos de Santos - SP." *Gremetal,* n.d. Web. 11 July 2014.

"'I Can't Feel My Legs': Neymar Sparked Brazil Panic after World Cup Injury." *The Sydney Morning Herald.* N.p., n.d. Web. 11 July 2014.

Kalliinho. "Neymar. The Story So Far. – ? || NEYMAR. The Story So Far • || 2013 HD ||

Klopman, Michael. "Neymar, Barcelona Agree to Five-Year Deal." *TheHuffingtonPost.com,* 26 May 2013. Web. 11 July 2014.

Koza, Norman. "Golden Shoes Soccer Movie." *Goldenshoesmovie.com,* 21 Mar. 2013. Web. 11 July 2014.

"Luciano Batista.com." *Luciano Batista.com.* N.p., n.d. Web. 11 July 2014.

"Globo Presents a Documentary About Neymar."
(n.d.): n. *Globo Presents: Globo TV Sports,*
Web. 11 Mar. 2013.

Matthias, B. S. "Neymar Is Ready for His
Home Debut at the Camp Nou."
www.unisportstore.com. Unisport,
2 Aug. 2013. Web. 11 July 2014.

"MINISTÉRIO PENIEL - Face a Face Com Deus."
MINISTÉRIO PENIEL - Face a Face Com Deus.
N.p., n.d. Web. 11 July 2014.

Mohamedmvp. "Neymar Is the Next Big Thing."
The Roar. N.p., 5 July 2013. Web. 11 July 2014.

"Neymar: All about the New 21 Years "messiah"
of BarÃ§a!" *Modernghana.com.* 29 May 2013.
Web. 11 July 2014.

"Neymar." *Biography, Stats, Rating, Footballer's
Profile.* Footballtop.com, n.d., Web. 11 July 2014.

"Neymar - Steps to a Great Player (Full Documentary)."
YouTube. 25 June 2013. Web. 11 July 2014.

"Neymar Biography." *Neymar.* Neymarbrazil.net,
2013. Web. 11 July 2014.

"Neymar Commits to Joining Barça in July."
MARCA.com (English Version). O Globo, n.d.
Web. 11 July 2014.

"Neymar da Silva Santos Jr." *Bio.com.* A&E
Television Networks, n.d. Web. 11 July 2014.

"Neymar Jr. - Win FIFA Goal of the Year - 2011."
YouTube. Eurosport Live, 9 Jan. 2012. Web.
11 July 2014.

"Neymar na Portuguesa Santista." *YouTube.* n.d.
Web. 11 July 2014.

"Neymar Posts Heartfelt Message about His
Father." *Sambafoot.com,* N.p., n.d. Web.
11 July 2014.

"Neymar Voted South America's Best Player."
Football News. NDTV Sports, 1 Jan. 2013.
Web. 11 July 2014.

"Neymar." *Wikipedia.* Wikimedia Foundation,
07 Nov. 2014. Web. 11 July 2014.

"[Neymar's AMAZING GOAL] Neymar Jr -
Winner The FIFA Puskas Award 2011 Best
Goal." *YouTube.* 10 Jan. 2012. Web.
11 July 2014.

"Paulo Henrique Ganso." *Wikipedia.* Wikimedia
Foundation, 07 Oct. 2014. Web. 11 July 2014.

Ramos, Raphael. "Neymar, a Origem do Mito nas Quadras de Santos - Esportes - Estadão" *Esportes.estadao.com.br.* 13 May 2012. Web. 11 July 2014.

Ravey. "The Trajectory of a Soccer Star - Neymar." *Soccer Talk.* 6 Nov. 2011. Web. 11 July 2014.

Reporter, Sportsmail. "Brazilian Wonderkid Neymar Wins 2011 Goal of the Year at Ballon D'Or Gala." *Mail Online.* Associated Newspapers, n.d. Web. 11 July 2014.

Reuters. "Neymar Living the Dream with Idol Messi at Barca - World - Sports - Ahram Online." Ahramonline, 1 Aug. 2013. Web. 11 July 2014.

"Rivais na Segunda Divisão Jabuca e Briosa já contaram com Neymar." *Chico sabe tudo.* N.p., n.d. Web. 11 July 2014.

"Santos FC História de Glórias.": *Neymar iniciou no Jabaquara e Portuguesa Santista.* N.p., 4 June 2012. Web. 11 July 2014.

"Sociedade Esportiva Palmeiras." *Wikipedia.* Wikimedia Foundation, 07 Dec. 2014. Web. 11 July 2014.

"Tici Pinheiros Entrevista Neymar - Programa Da
    Tarde 26/02/2013." *YouTube.* Novo Canal
    Oficial, 26 Feb. 2013. Web. 11 July 2014.

"To Read Exclusive Fans Content You Must Sign
    In." *Neymar Jr.* FC Barcelona, n.d. Web.
    11 July 2014.

Wright, Chris. "Neymar Will Not Be Joining
    Chelsea Any Time Soon." Who Ate All the Pies
    RSS. 14 Dec. 2010. Web. 11 July 2014.

The Flea – The Amazing Story of Leo Messi

By Michael Part

The captivating story of soccer legend Lionel Messi, from his first touch at age five in the streets of Rosario, Argentina, to his first goal on the Camp Nou pitch in Barcelona, Spain. *The Flea* tells the amazing story of a boy who was born to play the beautiful game and destined to become the world's greatest soccer player. The best-selling book by Michael Part is a must read for every soccer fan!

Ages 9 and up

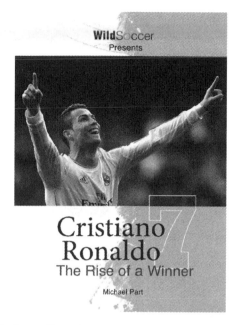

WildSoccer
Presents

Cristiano
Ronaldo
The Rise of a Winner

Michael Part

Cristiano Ronaldo – The Rise of a Winner

By Michael Part

Cristiano Ronaldo: The Rise of a Winner is the gripping life story of a boy who rose from the streets of Madeira to become one of the greatest soccer players ever. This heartfelt, stirring tale chronicles Ronaldo's road to glory, a journey that made him the man he is today.

Michael Part is the author of *The Flea: The Amazing Story of Leo Messi, The Pope Who Loves Soccer,* and the Disney classic *A Kid in King Arthur's Court.*

Ages 9 and up

HAVE YOU READ THE FIRST BOOK?
GET IT NOW!

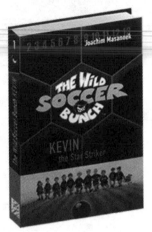

THE WILD SOCCER BUNCH
BOOK 1
KEVIN the Star Striker

When the last of the snow has finally melted, soccer season starts!

Kevin the Star Striker and the *Wild Soccer Bunch* rush to their field. They have found that Mickey the bulldozer and his gang, the *Unbeatables*, have taken over. Kevin and his friends challenge the *Unbeatables* to the biggest game of their lives.

Can the *Wild Soccer Bunch* defeat the *Unbeatables*, or will they lose their field of dreams forever? Can they do what no team has done before?

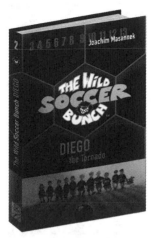

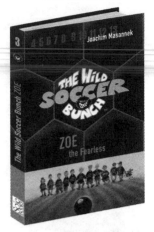

THE WILD SOCCER BUNCH
BOOK 3
ZOE the Fearless

Zoe is ten and soccer crazy. She spends each day dreaming of becoming the first woman to play for the U.S. Men's National Soccer Team. Her dad believes in her dream, and encourages her to join the *Wild Soccer Bunch*. Even though Zoe would be the only girl on the team, she knows she could be their best player. But the *Wild Bunch* is not open-minded when it comes to welcoming new teammates, especially when they are girls...

Zoe's dad has a plan. He organizes a birthday tournament and invites the *Wild Bunch*. They present Zoe with a pair of red high heels, expecting her to make a fool of herself during the tournament. Zoe gladly accepts her gift. She wears the heels during the biggest game of her life, and proves that she's got what it takes to be a wild, winning member of the *Wild Soccer Bunch*.

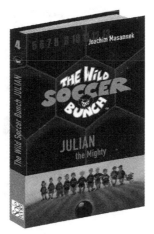

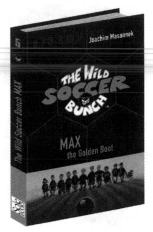

THE WILD SOCCER BUNCH
BOOK 5
MAX the Golden Boot

The championship game pits Max the golden boot and his team against the *Wild Soccer Bunch*. Max is so hooked by their attacking game that he dreams of being one of them. Although he is an amazing player, Danny and Kevin don't want him on the team. A power struggle ensues and threatens to break up and destroy the *Wild Soccer Bunch* who are on their top of their game.

INDEX

Page numbers in **bold** indicate photographs